SEAFOOD

LOVERS

COOK BOOK

**GOLDEN
WEST** ☼
PUBLISHERS

Back cover photo by David B. Moore, courtesy Antoinette Metzger and Chef Matthew Long of Steamers Genuine Seafood, Phoenix, AZ

Our sincere thanks to the following organizations:
Alaska Seafood Marketing Institute <alaskaseafood.org>
California Seafood Council <ca-seafood.org>
Casey's Seafood, Newport News, VA
Charleston Seafood <charlestonseafood.com>
National Fisheries Institute <nfi.org>
McCormick & Schmick's Seafood Restaurant, Portland, OR
Maine Lobster Promotion Council <mainelobsterpromo.com>
Maryland Department of Agriculture <mda.state.md.us/aqua>
Pacific Northwest Seafood Association <seafoodoregon.org>

Printed in the United States

2nd Printing © 2002

ISBN #1-885590-82-2

Golden West Publishers, Inc.
4113 N. Longview Ave.
Phoenix, AZ 85014, USA
(602) 265-4392

Visit our website: www.goldenwestpublishers.com

Seafood Lovers Cook Book

Table of Contents

Seafood Appetizers

Seafood Soups Stews & Chowders

Seafood Salads

Table of Contents (continued)

Introduction

Featuring recipes from the Atlantic to the Pacific and Alaska to the Gulf of Mexico, **Seafood Lovers Cook Book** offers mouth-watering dishes and a medley of seafood favorites. Whether you favor fish, shrimp, clams, oysters or lobster, **Seafood Lovers** has the recipe for you. From quick and easy meals to fabulous feasts, **Seafood Lovers Cook Book** offers you fine seafood dining experiences.

Seafood provides a high protein, low fat diet that is delicious and contributes to healthy living. Additionally, there is significant evidence that seafood's beneficial omega-3 fatty acids help to reduce heart disease. Research has also shown that fish contains no saturated fats, is rich in the desirable polyunsaturated fats and possesses large deposits of essential vitamins and minerals.

Whether recreating a coastal dining experience or preparing a simple backyard barbecue, the savory dishes in **Seafood Lovers Cook Book** will help you enjoy the sensible luxury of seafood!

Fish Substitution Chart

Thin, lean, white meat with a delicate flavor:
Flounder, Orange Roughy, Pompano, Snapper, Sole.

Medium-dense, light meat with a mild to moderate flavor:
Black Drum, Black Sea Bass, Butterfish, Catfish, Cod, Croaker, Grouper, Haddock, Monkfish, Pike, Pollock, Rainbow Trout, Redfish, Sablefish, Salmon, Scup, Sea Trout, Spot, Striped Bass, Tautog, Tilefish, Whitefish, White Perch, Whiting.

Medium-dense, darker meat with a more pronounced flavor:
Amberjack, Atlantic Mackerel, Bluefish, Bonita, Mullet, Ocean Trout, Shad, Tuna.

Thick, meat-like texture with distinct yet moderate flavor:
Halibut, Mahi Mahi, Marlin, Shark, Sturgeon, Swordfish.

Seafood Tips

When Buying Seafood

When food shopping, purchase seafood last and have it packed on ice for the trip home.

Storing Seafood

Store seafood in leak-proof containers for no more than two or three days in refrigerator or three to ten months frozen.

Storing Oysters and Clams

Never store live oysters or clams in airtight containers. Refrigerate for no more than five days. Both will naturally open during storage. Tap the shell lightly. If they do not close, they are dead and must be discarded.

Prevent Cross-Contamination

Wash hands before and after handling raw seafood; do not drip seafood juices on counters, utensils or other foods; thoroughly wash containers that held raw seafood.

Marinating Seafood

Always marinate seafood in the refrigerator.

Cooking Fresh Fish

In general, fish should be cooked for ten minutes per inch at 400° to 450°, turning the fish halfway through the total cooking time. If fish is cooked in a sauce or foil, add five minutes to the cooking time.

Cooking Frozen Fish

Double all cooking times if cooking unthawed fish.

Cooking Shrimp & Scallops

Shrimp and scallops become opaque and firm when fully cooked.

Cooking Oysters & Clams

Oysters and clams should be steamed or broiled until shells pop open; fried in oil for three to four minutes at 375°; or baked for ten minutes at 450°.

Seafood Appetizers

Crabmeat Snacks

Filling:
- 1 can (8 oz.) CRABMEAT, drained
- 2 Tbsp. chopped PIMENTO
- 1 HARD-BOILED EGG, chopped
- 1 Tbsp. chopped ONION
- 1/3 cup chopped CELERY
- 1/2 tsp. SALT
- 1/3 cup MAYONNAISE

Pastry:
- 2 cups FLOUR*
- 1 tsp. SALT
- 2/3 cup + 2 Tbsp. SHORTENING
- 4-5 Tbsp. COLD WATER

Combine filling ingredients, cover and refrigerate. In a large bowl, combine flour and salt. Cut in shortening thoroughly. Sprinkle in water, 1 tablespoon at a time, mixing until all flour is moistened. Gather dough into a ball, divide in half and roll out to the thickness of a pie crust on a lightly floured board. With a cookie cutter, cut out 16 (2-inch) circles; place 1 tablespoon of crabmeat filling in the center of each. Moisten edges and cover with circles cut from the remaining dough. Press edges with tines of a fork to seal. Place on an ungreased baking sheet and prick tops several times with a fork. Bake at 425° for 20-25 minutes.

*If using self-rising flour, omit salt from pastry.

Mexican Seafood Dip

1 can (15 oz.) PINTO BEANS, drained and rinsed
1 Tbsp. + 1 tsp. TACO SEASONING MIX
2 Tbsp. FAT FREE SOUR CREAM
1 ripe AVOCADO
1 Tbsp. LIME JUICE
1 Tbsp. FAT FREE MAYONNAISE
1/4 tsp. WORCESTERSHIRE SAUCE
1/8 tsp. CHILI POWDER
1/8 tsp. GARLIC POWDER
8 oz. flake style CRAB or LOBSTER
    FLAVOR SURIMI
3 Tbsp. sliced BLACK OLIVES
1/2 sm. TOMATO, chopped
1/4 cup CORN
1/2 cup shredded SHARP CHEDDAR CHEESE
2 Tbsp. chopped GREEN ONION TOPS

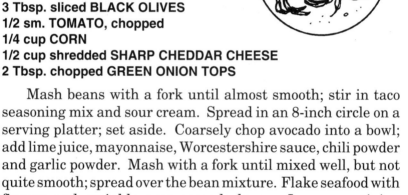

Mash beans with a fork until almost smooth; stir in taco seasoning mix and sour cream. Spread in an 8-inch circle on a serving platter; set aside. Coarsely chop avocado into a bowl; add lime juice, mayonnaise, Worcestershire sauce, chili powder and garlic powder. Mash with a fork until mixed well, but not quite smooth; spread over the bean mixture. Flake seafood with fingers and sprinkle over avocado layer. Layer remaining ingredients in the order listed. Cover and refrigerate until ready to serve, up to 2 hours. Let stand at room temperature for 15 minutes before serving. Serve with salsa and tortilla chips.

Surimi

Surimi (formed fish) *has been made for centuries by the Japanese. Most North American surimi is made from Alaska pollock, a fish with a lean, firm flesh that has a delicate, slightly sweet flavor. The pollock is processed to a paste and then flavor concentrates from the real shellfish are added. The mixture is then formed into the shellfish it is representing and color is added.*

Clam Dip with Vegetables

1 can (6.5 oz.) minced CLAMS
1 cup LIGHT SOUR CREAM
1 Tbsp. minced fresh CHIVES or 1 tsp. dried CHIVES
1 tsp. LEMON JUICE
1/8 tsp. HOT PEPPER SAUCE
Whole CHIVES for garnish
4 lg. CARROTS, cut into dipping sticks
5 oz. CHINESE PEA PODS, stems and strings removed
ASSORTED CRACKERS

Drain clams, reserving liquid. In a small bowl, combine sour cream, chives, lemon juice and hot pepper sauce. Stir in clams and 1 tablespoon of the reserved liquid (or enough to make the consistency of a dip); mix well. Garnish with whole chives and serve with carrots, pea pods and crackers.

Corn & Shrimp Dip

1 cup frozen CORN
3 Tbsp. chopped GREEN BELL PEPPER
3 Tbsp. chopped RED BELL PEPPER
1 tsp. VEGETABLE OIL
3/4 cup shredded SHARP CHEDDAR CHEESE
1/2 cup LOW FAT SOUR CREAM
8 oz. cooked SALAD SHRIMP
1 Tbsp. LIME JUICE
Fresh CILANTRO for garnish
MELBA TOAST, CRACKERS or TORTILLA CHIPS

Combine corn, bell peppers and oil in a shallow baking pan. Bake at 425° for 20-25 minutes, stirring occasionally, until vegetables are lightly browned. Transfer vegetables to a saucepan, stir in cheese, sour cream and shrimp. Cook over low heat, stirring frequently, until cheese melts; do not boil. Stir in lime juice. Transfer to a chafing dish to keep warm. Garnish with cilantro and serve with melba toast, crackers or tortilla chips.

Crunchy Crab Cakes

1 lb. CRABMEAT
1 Tbsp. minced GREEN BELL PEPPER
1 Tbsp. minced ONION
3/4 tsp. MUSTARD
1/2 tsp. SALT
Dash of PEPPER
1 tsp. OLD BAY® SEASONING
2-3 drops WORCESTERSHIRE SAUCE

Sauce:
  2 Tbsp. BUTTER
  1 1/2 Tbsp. FLOUR
  1/3 cup MILK

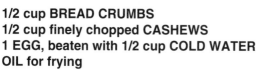

1/2 cup BREAD CRUMBS
1/2 cup finely chopped CASHEWS
1 EGG, beaten with 1/2 cup COLD WATER
OIL for frying

In a large bowl, combine the first 8 ingredients and toss gently; set aside. In a saucepan over medium heat, combine and cook the sauce ingredients until thickened. Combine sauce with crabmeat mixture and form into small patties. In a shallow dish, mix bread crumbs and cashews. Coat patties with bread crumbs, dip into egg mixture, then coat again with bread crumbs. Fry in hot oil until golden brown.

Cajun Dip

1/2 lb. cooked SHRIMP, SCALLOPS
  or OYSTERS, chopped
12-20 oz. MEDIUM or HOT SALSA
Pinch of GARLIC POWDER

Pinch of PEPPER
4 Tbsp. SOUR CREAM
2 Tbsp. CILANTRO

In a medium bowl, mix seafood, salsa, garlic and pepper. Chill for at least 1 hour to blend flavors. Spoon into a serving bowl, top with sour cream and sprinkle with cilantro. Serve with tortilla chips, potato chips or crackers.

Red Snapper Dip

**3/4 lb. RED SNAPPER, TILEFISH, AMBERJACK, GROUPER or
SHARK, cooked and flaked
1 can (10.75 oz.) CREAM OF SHRIMP SOUP
1 pkg. (8 oz.) CREAM CHEESE, softened
1 tsp. LEMON JUICE
2 Tbsp. chopped PARSLEY
1/4 tsp. GARLIC POWDER
1/4 tsp. PAPRIKA
Fresh PARSLEY SPRIGS for garnish
ASSORTED CRACKERS**

In a medium bowl, combine all ingredients, except parsley sprigs and crackers. Cover and chill at least 1 hour to blend flavors. Garnish with parsley sprigs and serve with assorted crackers.

Marinated Crabmeat Dip

**1 lb. CRABMEAT
1/3 cup finely chopped ONION**

**Vinaigrette:
1/4 cup VEGETABLE OIL
1/4 cup WATER
1/2 cup CIDER VINEGAR
1 Tbsp. SEAFOOD SEASONING
1 Tbsp. chopped fresh PARSLEY**

Carefully sort crabmeat and remove any cartilage. Gently mix onion into the crabmeat. In a small bowl, combine the vinaigrette ingredients and pour over the crabmeat. Cover and refrigerate for at least 2 hours.   Serve with your favorite crackers.

Oyster-Stuffed Eggs

12 HARD-BOILED EGGS
4 GREEN ONIONS, minced
2 Tbsp. BUTTER
12 OYSTERS, chopped,
    liquor reserved

2 cloves GARLIC, minced
1 Tbsp. minced CELERY LEAVES
3 Tbsp. BREAD CRUMBS
1 tsp. minced PARSLEY
SALT and PEPPER to taste

Cut eggs lengthwise; remove and mash yolks. Sauté onions in butter until soft; add oysters, garlic and celery leaves. Cook slowly until liquid evaporates. Remove from heat, stir in bread crumbs, parsley, salt and pepper. Add to yolks and mix well. Moisten with oyster liquor if too dry. Mound mixture in egg white shells, sprinkle with parsley and brown in a 350° oven for 10-15 minutes.

Dungeness Crabs
This highly prized crab can be found on the Pacific coast from Mexico to Alaska.

Dungeness Delightful Dip

1/2 lb. DUNGENESS CRABMEAT
1/2 Tbsp. LEMON JUICE
2 Tbsp. OLIVE OIL
SALT to taste
WHITE PEPPER or TABASCO®
1 Tbsp. finely minced SHALLOTS
    or GREEN ONIONS
2-3 Tbsp. minced fresh PARSLEY,
    TARRAGON, BASIL or CHIVES
1/4 cup MAYONNAISE
SALAD GREENS

In a large mixing bowl, season crabmeat with lemon juice, oil, salt, pepper, shallots and herbs; toss lightly. Let stand at least 20 minutes to absorb the flavor of the seasonings. Before serving, drain excess liquid and toss with just enough mayonnaise to lightly coat the crabmeat. Serve on a bed of salad greens.

Crabmeat Spring Rolls with Plum Dipping Sauce

3/4 cup CRABMEAT, flaked
1/2 cup minced CABBAGE
1/3 cup chopped cooked GREEN BEANS
1/3 cup chopped uncooked BEAN SPROUTS
2 Tbsp. chopped canned BAMBOO SHOOTS
1-2 tsp. minced PICKLED GINGER
1 Tbsp. chopped GREEN ONIONS
2 Tbsp. grated CARROT
1-2 tsp. chopped CILANTRO
SPRING ROLL WRAPPERS

In a medium bowl, combine all ingredients, except wrappers; mix well. Place 3 tablespoons of filling on front section of a spring roll wrapper. Form the filling to a 3-inch by 1 1/2-inch mound. Fold one end of the wrapper over the filling, then fold the 2 sides toward the middle. Roll the wrapper up and place seam side down on a platter. Slice spring rolls in half and serve with warm *Plum Dipping Sauce,* or leave whole and fry in hot oil until golden brown.

Makes 7 spring rolls.

Note: Spring roll wrappers (lumpia) may be found in the frozen food section of Asian food stores and in some supermarkets. Rice paper wrappers may also be used, although they are more difficult to handle. Won ton wrappers may be substituted, but these must be cooked, as they are a noodle.

Plum Dipping Sauce

2 Tbsp. PLUM JELLY
1 tsp. SOY SAUCE
2 tsp. RICE VINEGAR

In a saucepan, combine plum jelly, soy sauce and rice vinegar. Heat over low heat until jelly is melted.

Blue Crabmeat Appetizers

The following eight appetizers will use this base.

2 cups BLUE CRABMEAT
1/2 cup finely chopped RED and GREEN
    BELL PEPPERS
1/2 cup finely chopped GREEN ONIONS
1/2 tsp. minced GARLIC
1 tsp. minced PARSLEY
1/4 cup MAYONNAISE
1 tsp. SEAFOOD SEASONING

Combine all ingredients and mix thoroughly.

Makes 3 1/4 cups *Blue Crabmeat Base.*

Blue Crabmeat Dijon Dip

1 pkg. (8 oz.) CREAM CHEESE, softened
3/4 cup SOUR CREAM
1 tsp. DIJON MUSTARD
3 1/4 cups BLUE CRABMEAT BASE
COCONUT FLAKES

In a medium bowl, blend cream cheese, sour cream and mustard with an electric mixer until smooth. Add *Blue Crabmeat Base* and stir. Chill thoroughly. Pour into a glass serving bowl, sprinkle with coconut and serve with vegetable dippers.

Stuffed Tomatoes

32 CHERRY TOMATOES
3 1/4 cups BLUE CRABMEAT BASE
1/4 cup chopped CELERY
2 tsp. LEMON JUICE

Cut tops off the tomatoes, remove seeds and place upside down on paper towels to drain. In a small bowl, combine crabmeat base, celery and lemon juice; mix well. Stuff tomatoes with crabmeat mixture. Chill and serve.

Tortilla Roll-Ups

1 pkg. (8 oz.) CREAM CHEESE, softened
1 cup SOUR CREAM
1 jar (4 oz.) PIMENTOS, finely chopped
1 can (4 oz.) GREEN CHILES, finely chopped
1 cup shredded CHEDDAR CHEESE
3 1/4 cups BLUE CRABMEAT BASE (p. 14)
8 FLOUR TORTILLAS

In a bowl, combine all ingredients except tortillas and mix well. Spread the mixture on the tortillas; roll up each tortilla and wrap in plastic wrap. Refrigerate for several hours. When ready to serve, slice tortillas into 6-8 slices.

Makes 48-64 roll-ups.

Stuffed Mushrooms

50 med. MUSHROOMS
1 pkg. (8 oz.) CREAM CHEESE, softened
3 1/4 cups BLUE CRABMEAT BASE (p. 14)
Grated PARMESAN CHEESE

Remove stems from mushrooms. In a bowl, combine cream cheese with the **Blue Crabmeat Base.** Stuff mushroom caps with the mixture and sprinkle with Parmesan cheese. Place on a cookie sheet and broil until tops are golden brown.

Blue Crab Bites

3 1/4 cups BLUE CRABMEAT BASE (p. 14)
1/4 cup finely chopped CELERY
2 tsp. SEAFOOD SEASONING
1 cup MATZO MEAL
1 EGG, beaten
OIL for frying
SEAFOOD COCKTAIL SAUCE

In a bowl, combine **Blue Crabmeat Base,** celery, seafood seasoning and 1/2 of the matzo meal. Form mixture into 35 balls, then roll balls in remaining matzo meal. Fry in oil heated to 375° until brown. Serve with seafood cocktail sauce.

Crispy Won Tons

3 1/4 cups BLUE CRABMEAT BASE (p. 14)　**OIL for frying**
3/4 tsp. grated GINGERROOT　**SWEET AND SOUR**
8 WATER CHESTNUTS, finely chopped　**SAUCE**
16 WON TON WRAPPERS　**HOT MUSTARD**

In a medium bowl, combine *Blue Crabmeat Base,* ginger-root and water chestnuts. Cut won ton wrappers into four equal pieces. Place one teaspoon of the crabmeat mixture in the center of each piece. Moisten edges of wrapper with water. Fold lengthwise edges over center, then fold crosswise edges over center; press to seal, using more water if necessary. Fry in 375° oil until brown and crispy. Serve with sweet and sour sauce and hot mustard.

Makes 64.

Ravioli Supreme

3 1/4 cups BLUE CRABMEAT BASE (p. 14)　**TOMATO SAUCE**
36 WON TON WRAPPERS　**PARMESAN CHEESE**

Place small amounts of *Blue Crabmeat Base* on half of the wrappers. Moisten the remaining wrappers and place on top. Cut into squares or rounds, centered around the filling, then moisten edges and seal tightly. Cook a few at a time in 1 1/2 quarts of boiling salted water for 4-5 minutes; remove with a slotted spoon. Serve with tomato sauce and Parmesan cheese.

Hawaiian Delight

3 1/4 cups BLUE CRABMEAT BASE (p. 14)
1/4 cup crushed PINEAPPLE
1/4 cup chopped MANGO
COCONUT FLAKES

In a bowl, combine *Blue Crabmeat Base,* pineapple and mango. Place approximately 2 tablespoons of the mixture in each of 24-28 small crab shells. Sprinkle with coconut. Bake at 350° for 15 minutes; serve warm.

Seaside Nachos

1/2 bag (14 oz.) baked TORTILLA CHIPS
1 can (16 oz.) REFRIED BEANS
2 Tbsp. PICANTE SAUCE
1 1/2 Tbsp. LIME JUICE
8 oz. CRABMEAT or flake style CRAB
    FLAVORED SURIMI
2 cups grated CHEESE

Toppings:
    GUACAMOLE, SOUR CREAM, chopped TOMATOES

Spread chips in a single layer in a 15 x 10 pan; set aside. In a small bowl, combine refried beans, picante sauce and lime juice and stir well. Spread bean mixture onto each chip. Sprinkle seafood evenly over chips and top with cheese. Bake at 375° for 8-10 minutes or until cheese melts. Serve with desired toppings.

Did You Know?
Shrimp generally swim forward, but can swim backward by simply flipping their fan-shaped tails.

Spicy Steamed Shrimp

1 lb. med. SHRIMP, in the shell
2 tsp. OIL

Seasoning:
    1 1/2 tsp. CELERY SALT
    3/4 tsp. PAPRIKA
    3/4 tsp. DRY MUSTARD
    1/8 tsp. CAYENNE

Place shrimp in a bowl, drizzle with oil and toss lightly. In another bowl, combine seasoning ingredients. Add to shrimp and mix gently. Place shrimp on a steamer rack over boiling water. Reduce heat and steam, covered, for 2-3 minutes or until bright pink and opaque throughout. Serve warm with your favorite spicy cocktail sauce.

Smoked Salmon-Caper Ball

1 pkg. (8 oz.) CREAM CHEESE, softened
1 Tbsp. LEMON JUICE
1 Tbsp. MILK
1 Tbsp. CAPERS, drained and rinsed
1 cup SMOKED SALMON
1/4 cup chopped fresh PARSLEY
LETTUCE

Combine cream cheese, lemon juice, milk and capers with 2/3 cup of salmon in a food processor or blender; mix until smooth. Add remaining 1/3 cup of salmon and mix in lightly. Chill in a small bowl lined with plastic wrap. Just before serving, form into a ball, roll in parsley and place on serving plate on a bed of lettuce. Serve with your favorite crackers.

Did You Know?
Salmon are high in protein and are a rich source of vitamin A, the B-group vitamins and Omega-3 oils.

Baked Oysters

24 SELECT or EXTRA-SELECT
  OYSTERS, shucked
1/2 cup FLOUR
1 tsp. SALT

1/8 tsp. PEPPER
2 EGGS, slightly beaten
1/2 cup BUTTER, melted
LEMON WEDGES

Preheat oven to 425°. Drain oysters and dry slightly with paper towels. In a shallow dish, mix flour, salt and pepper. Roll oysters in the flour mixture, dip in eggs, then roll in the flour mixture again. Arrange in a greased, shallow baking dish and pour butter over each. Bake for 10-15 minutes or until lightly browned; baste twice while baking. Garnish with lemon wedges.

Oysters Casino

24 EXTRA-SELECT OYSTERS, shucked
6 slices BACON
1/2 cup finely chopped ONION
1/4 cup finely chopped CELERY
1/4 cup finely chopped GREEN BELL PEPPER
2 tsp. LEMON JUICE
1/2 tsp. SALT
1 tsp. WORCESTERSHIRE SAUCE
6 drops TABASCO®

Thaw oysters and rinse thoroughly. Preheat oven to 400°. In a medium skillet, partially cook bacon. Add onion, celery, and bell pepper to the skillet and sauté until tender. Stir in lemon juice, salt, Worcestershire sauce and Tabasco. Arrange oysters on a baking sheet and divide bacon mixture evenly over tops of each. Bake for 10-12 minutes or until edges of oysters begin to curl and the topping is brown.

Blue Crab Fingers & Mustard Sauce

Mustard Sauce:
1 cup MAYONNAISE
1 tsp. WORCESTERSHIRE SAUCE
2 Tbsp. MUSTARD
1/4 tsp. DRY MUSTARD

2 cans BLUE CRAB FINGERS (cocktail claws: 40-50 per can)

In a small bowl, combine all sauce ingredients and whip until smooth. Serve with blue crab fingers.

Oysters Brochette

12 OYSTERS, drained   12 slices BACON   4 slices TOAST

Wrap each oyster in a slice of bacon and skewer with a toothpick. Bake in a 350° oven until bacon is done (about 15 minutes). Serve on toast tips.

Broiled Breaded Oysters

24 EXTRA-SELECT OYSTERS, shucked	1 cup fine dry BREAD CRUMBS
	SALT and PEPPER to taste
1 EGG	1/4 cup BUTTER, melted
3 tsp. MILK	LEMON WEDGES

Grease a shallow baking pan with butter. Drain oysters and dry on paper towels. Combine the egg with milk and beat lightly. Place bread crumbs in a shallow dish and combine with salt and pepper. Dip each oyster in egg mixture, then roll in the bread crumbs to coat. Arrange oysters in prepared baking pan and drizzle melted butter over each. Broil 2 inches from the broiler unit for 2-3 minutes. Remove the pan, turn oysters over, add more butter and broil other side until browned. Serve with lemon wedges.

How To Shuck An Oyster

Hold oyster firmly in your hand with your palm protected by a towel. With your other hand, insert the tip of an oyster knife near the oyster's hinge. Twist and turn gently to pop the shell open, being careful not to fracture the shell. Once opened, use your knife to slide under and over oyster meat, cutting the connections holding it in place.

Deviled Oysters

18 SELECT or EXTRA-SELECT OYSTERS, shucked
1 cup condensed CREAM OF MUSHROOM SOUP
1 tsp. WORCESTERSHIRE SAUCE
1/2 tsp. DRY MUSTARD
2 tsp. LEMON JUICE
1/2 cup fine dry BREAD CRUMBS
2 Tbsp. BUTTER or MARGARINE

Preheat oven to 400°. Grease 6 small baking dishes with butter. Wash oysters, chop coarsely and mix with soup, Worcestershire sauce, mustard and lemon juice. Spoon mixture into baking dishes; top with bread crumbs and dot with butter. Bake for 12-15 minutes.

Dungeness Crab Phyllo

1 lb. DUNGENESS CRABMEAT
1 1/2 cups BÉARNAISE SAUCE
1 pkg. (16 oz.) frozen PHYLLO DOUGH
1/2 cup BUTTER, melted
1/2 cup seasoned BREAD CRUMBS
ICE WATER

Preheat oven to 400°. Lightly grease a baking sheet. Combine crabmeat with *Béarnaise Sauce;* set aside. Place first leaf of phyllo dough on baking sheet and brush with melted butter; sprinkle with bread crumbs. Repeat this process with seven to ten more leaves. Spread crab mixture evenly over top leaf. Begin layering phyllo as before on top of crab mixture. Pile phyllo, butter and bread crumbs seven to ten leaves high. Mold sides shut with ice water. Brush top with remaining butter and bake in the middle of the oven for 30 minutes or until top is golden brown.

Béarnaise Sauce

3/4 cup WHITE WINE
1 1/2 tsp. chopped fresh TARRAGON leaves
1 1/2 tsp. chopped fresh CHERVIL leaves
3 GREEN ONIONS (white only), sliced
12 EGG YOLKS
3 Tbsp. COLD WATER
3 sticks BUTTER, softened
SALT and PEPPER to taste

Combine wine, tarragon, chervil and onions in a small saucepan and bring to a boil. Lower heat and let bubble until liquid is reduced by half. Strain through cheesecloth and cool. In the top of a double boiler, beat egg yolks on high speed with electric mixer until thick. Stir in water and place pan over simmering water. Heat, stirring constantly with a wooden spoon until egg mixture is warm. Add butter a little at a time, stirring constantly. When mixture coats a metal spoon remove from heat and add salt and pepper to taste. Gradually add wine mixture and blend.

Makes 1 1/2 cups.

Lemon Yogurt Seafood Dip

1 cup LEMON YOGURT
1 tsp. LIME JUICE
2 Tbsp. puréed CHUTNEY

3 shakes TABASCO®
1 Tbsp. chopped fresh MINT
SEAFOOD of choice

In a bowl, combine yogurt, lime juice, chutney, Tabasco and mint. Cover and chill overnight. Serve with cooked and chunked fish, shrimp, crab, etc.

Tasty Sardine Bits

2 cans (3.75 oz. ea.) boneless, skinless SARDINES
BATTER of choice (see p. 89)
1/2 cup crushed CORNFLAKES
BUTTER

Drain sardines and then dip each in batter. Coat with cornflakes and sauté in butter for 5 minutes or until golden brown.

Lobster Puffs

2 cups FLOUR
1/2 tsp. SALT
Several dashes CAYENNE
3 tsp. BAKING POWDER

1 EGG, well-beaten
1 cup MILK
1/2 lb. chopped LOBSTER MEAT
2 cups PEANUT OIL

In a large mixing bowl, sift together flour, salt, cayenne and baking powder. In another bowl, blend together egg and milk; stir in lobster meat. Add lobster mixture to flour mixture and mix well. Heat the peanut oil in a large skillet until hot, but not smoking, or in an electric fryer set at 365°. Carefully drop the lobster mixture by rounded tablespoon into the hot oil and fry 3 minutes or until golden. Drain on paper towels. Serve with **Tartar Sauce** (see p. 85).

Lobster & Shrimp Cocktail

1 1/2 lbs. diced LOBSTER MEAT
1 1/2 lbs. SHRIMP, cooked
1 head ROMAINE LETTUCE, julienne

Dressing:
    1 cup MAYONNAISE
    2 cups SOUR CREAM
    1/2 Tbsp. CURRY
    2-3 Tbsp. CHUTNEY
    1 Tbsp. HORSERADISH
    1/2 tsp. grated LEMON or LIME PEEL

Fresh PARSLEY for garnish

In a bowl, combine all dressing ingredients; mix well. Arrange a bed of greens in cocktail glasses and distribute seafood between them. Dollop with dressing and garnish with parsley.

Did You Know?

Lobsters have one crusher claw that is heavy with thick teeth and one that is smaller with sharper teeth for tearing. However, not all lobsters have the heavy claw on the same side. Some are "right-handed" and others are "left-handed."

Lobster Paté

1 lb. finely diced LOBSTER MEAT
3 lbs. softened CREAM CHEESE
1 cup SOUR CREAM
2 Tbsp. each minced PARSLEY,
    CHIVES, TARRAGON
    and CHERVIL

JUICE of 1/2 LEMON
SALT and PEPPER to taste
LETTUCE
ASSORTED CRACKERS
VEGETABLE STICKS

Combine all ingredients in an electric mixer. Mix on low speed until thoroughly combined. Arrange a bed of lettuce on a serving platter and mold paté on top. Garnish platter with crackers and vegetables.

Oysters Rockefeller

3/4 cup BREAD CRUMBS
1/2 cup BUTTER, softened
1/2 pkg. (10 oz.) frozen chopped SPINACH
6 sm. GREEN ONIONS
2 stalks CELERY
1/3 bunch PARSLEY
1/3 head LETTUCE
1 Tbsp. WORCESTERSHIRE SAUCE
1 tsp. ANCHOVY PASTE
1/8 tsp. HOT SAUCE
1/4 tsp. SALT
1 1/2 Tbsp. ABSINTHE FLAVORED LIQUEUR
36 OYSTERS, shucked and drained
ROCK SALT
1/4 cup grated PARMESAN CHEESE

In a large bowl, combine 1/4 cup bread crumbs and butter; set aside. Place spinach, green onions, celery, parsley and lettuce in a blender container and purée. Fold spinach mixture into bread crumb mixture. Add Worcestershire sauce, anchovy paste, hot sauce, salt and liqueur and mix thoroughly. Place oysters on half shells and set in a pan of rock salt that has been heated for 20 minutes in a 450° oven. Spread 2 tablespoons of the spinach mixture over each oyster. In a separate bowl, combine remaining bread crumbs and Parmesan cheese; spread each oyster with 1 teaspoon of the cheese mixture. Bake for 30 minutes in a 450° oven, then broil 3 inches from heat, until top is golden brown.

Serves 6.

Oysters Rockefeller

This sumptuous dish was reportedly named for John D. Rockefeller who, in the late 1890s, was the world's richest man. Sometimes also known as "Oysters on the Half Shell," this tasty treat utilizes rock salt as a baking base so that the shells will not tip and spill their contents while baking.

Mardi Gras Oyster Stew

1 1/4 cups WATER
36 med. OYSTERS in liquor (about 18 oz.)
1 stick UNSALTED BUTTER
1 cup finely chopped CELERY
3/4 tsp. CHEF PAUL PRUDHOMME'S® SEAFOOD MAGIC
1/2 cup finely chopped GREEN ONIONS
2 cups HEAVY CREAM

In a large bowl, combine water and oysters and refrigerate at least 1 hour; strain and reserve the oysters and oyster water in the refrigerator until ready to use. In a large skillet, combine butter, celery, Seafood Magic and 3/4 cup of the oyster water. Cook over high heat for 3 minutes, shaking pan almost constantly instead of stirring. Add the remaining 1/2 cup oyster water and continue cooking and shaking the pan for 1 minute. Stir in green onions. Gradually add the cream, whisking constantly. Add oysters and cook for 2-4 minutes or just until the edges curl, whisking constantly. Remove from heat and serve immediately, stirring well as you ladle out portions.

Serves 4-5.

Oyster Calypso Stew

16 oz. fresh shucked OYSTERS, liquor reserved
1 tsp. LEMON JUICE
1/2-3/4 cup CLAM JUICE or CHICKEN STOCK
2 slices uncooked BACON, minced
1 cup thinly sliced MUSHROOMS
1/2 cup diced ONION
1/2 cup thinly sliced CELERY
1/2 cup small-diced CARROT
1/2 cup diced RED BELL PEPPER
1/2 cup DRY or MEDIUM-DRY SHERRY
1/2 tsp. THYME
1/4-1/2 tsp. TABASCO®
1 cup large-diced or quartered
   cooked RED POTATOES
1 Tbsp. CORNSTARCH
1 1/4 cups HALF AND HALF
SALT and PEPPER
1 Tbsp. chopped PARSLEY
LEMON WEDGES for garnish

Drain oysters, reserving liquor; set aside. Combine oyster liquor and lemon juice and add clam juice to make 3/4 cup total; set aside. In a large heavy saucepan or Dutch oven, sauté bacon over medium-high heat until about half-cooked (2-3 minutes). Add mushrooms, onion, celery, carrot and red pepper and reduce heat to medium. Sauté vegetable mixture about 4 minutes, stirring often. Stir in sherry and thyme, followed by the oyster liquor mixture, Tabasco and potatoes. Bring mixture to a boil. Stir cornstarch into half and half and whisk mixture into gently boiling stew. Add oysters immediately. Heat just until oysters get plump and their edges are ruffled (1-2 minutes). Season to taste with salt and pepper. Spoon stew into bowls and sprinkle with parsley. Serve with lemon wedges.

Did You Know?
Pearl oysters, certain freshwater mussels and abalone are all capable of producing valuable pearls.

Traditional Oyster Stew

1 pt. shucked OYSTERS, liquor reserved
4 cups MILK
1/4 cup MARGARINE or BUTTER
SALT and PEPPER to taste
SEAFOOD SEASONING

In a 4-quart pan, cook oysters with liquor over low heat until edges of oysters just begin to curl. Add milk, margarine, salt and pepper. Heat slowly until hot; do not boil. Serve with seafood seasoning on the side.

Serves 6.

Pearl Oysters

The inside of pearl oyster shells is covered with a smooth, shiny substance called mother-of-pearl *or* nacre. *If a grain of sand or other object gets into the body of a pearl oyster, the mantle covers it with thin layers of shell material and forms a pearl.*

Hearty Scallop Soup

2 cups MILK
1 cup HEAVY CREAM
2 Tbsp. BUTTER or MARGARINE
1 tsp. SALT
1/4 tsp. WHITE PEPPER
1 tsp. WORCESTERSHIRE SAUCE
1 lb. SCALLOPS, chopped into small pieces
PAPRIKA
3 Tbsp. finely chopped fresh PARSLEY

In the top of a double boiler, blend milk, cream, butter, salt, pepper and Worcestershire sauce. Place over boiling water and bring to a simmer, stirring frequently. Add scallops to the mixture and cook until tender, about 8-10 minutes. Pour hot soup into individual bowls; garnish with paprika and parsley.

Serves 6.

Seafood Gumbo

4-5 lbs. (10-12) CHICKEN THIGHS
1/4 cup OLIVE OIL
1 cup chopped ONION
1/2 cup chopped GREEN BELL PEPPER
1/3 cup FLOUR
2 cloves GARLIC, crushed
1 can (28 oz.) TOMATOES
2 cups CHICKEN BROTH or WATER
1/2 tsp. cracked RED PEPPER
1/2 tsp. THYME
1 BAY LEAF
1 pkg. (10 oz.) frozen sliced OKRA
1/2 pt. STANDARD OYSTERS
1 1/2 lbs. CRABMEAT
1/2 cup finely chopped fresh PARSLEY
Cooked RICE

Preheat oven to 350°. Place chicken thighs in a single layer in a shallow baking pan. Bake for 45-50 minutes or until juices run clear when pierced at the thickest part. Heat olive oil in the bottom of a large Dutch oven or heavy saucepan. Add onion and bell pepper and cook over medium-low heat for 10 minutes or until onion is translucent, stirring occasionally. Stir in flour, reduce heat to low and cook for 5 minutes. Add garlic, tomatoes, chicken broth, red pepper, thyme and bay leaf and cook, stirring constantly, until slightly thickened. Cover and cook over lowest heat for 30 minutes, stirring occasionally to prevent sticking. Add cooked chicken with pan juices and okra. Bring to a simmer and cook for 15-20 minutes. Stir in oysters, crabmeat and parsley and cook for 5-10 minutes or until seafood is heated thoroughly and the edges of the oysters begin to curl. Remove bay leaf. Serve in soup bowls over rice.

Serves 10-12.

Select or Standard?

Oysters are graded and sold by size, the largest are referred to as "select" and the average are called "standard."

Northwest Cioppino

1/4 cup VEGETABLE OIL
1 cup chopped ONION
2 cloves GARLIC, finely minced
1 can (8 oz.) TOMATO SAUCE
3 cups chopped fresh TOMATOES
1/2 cup DRY WHITE WINE
2 tsp. SALT
1 Tbsp. minced fresh SWEET BASIL
1 tsp. dried THYME
1 tsp. dried MARJORAM
1 tsp. dried OREGANO
1 BAY LEAF
1/4 tsp. PEPPER
4 WHOLE CLOVES
1 1/2 lbs. LIGHT MEAT FISH FILLETS*, cut into 1/2-inch pieces
1 dz. STEAMER CLAMS, scrubbed
1 whole cooked DUNGENESS CRAB
1 cup cooked SHRIMP
1/4 cup chopped fresh PARSLEY

In a large kettle, heat oil, add onion and garlic and sauté until onion is tender but not brown. Add tomato sauce, tomatoes, wine and all seasonings, except the parsley. Simmer for 20-30 minutes until desired thickness, stirring occasionally. Add pieces of fish and cook for 10 minutes. Add clams in the shell; cook until clams open. Remove crab from kettle; separate claws and quarter the remainder of the crab. Place all crab pieces in kettle and cook for 5 minutes; remove bay leaf. Just before serving, stir in shrimp and parsley.

Serves 8-10.

*See Fish Substitution Chart on page 5.

Cioppino

(chuh-PEE-noh)

San Francisco's Italian immigrants are credited with creating this delicious fish stew.

Bouillabaisse

2-3 Tbsp. OLIVE OIL
4 cloves GARLIC, minced
1 tsp. finely chopped fresh FENNEL
1/2 cup chopped ONION
1/2 cup chopped LEEKS
Pinch of SAFFRON
2 BAY LEAVES, crushed
SALT and PEPPER to taste
1 lb. ea. COD, SWORDFISH, CLAMS,
    MUSSELS, WHITE SEABASS, SEA
    SCALLOPS, cleaned and deboned
1 lg. CRAB, cracked and portioned
1 SPINY LOBSTER TAIL, cut into pieces
8 lg. SPOT PRAWNS or 12-20 RIDGEBACK
    PRAWNS
6 oz. CALAMARI (squid) rings and
    tentacles, cleaned
8 cups FISH STOCK
GARLIC CROUTONS
Fresh, crusty FRENCH BREAD

In a large skillet, heat olive oil and sauté garlic, fennel, onion, leeks, saffron, bay leaves, and salt and pepper until onion is translucent; set aside. Cut all fish into 1-inch cubes, scrub all of the shellfish. Place seafood, fish stock and sautéed vegetable mixture in a 6-quart saucepan. Cook over high heat for 20-25 minutes or until clams open. Serve in individual soup bowls; sprinkle with croutons. Serve with French bread.

Serves 8-12.

Bouillabaisse
(bool-yah-BEHZ)

This celebrated stew is from Provence, France. It is traditionally served with thick, crusty slices of French bread.

Lobster Bisque

2 Tbsp. QUICK COOKING TAPIOCA	1 Tbsp. minced ONION
1 1/4 tsp. SALT	3 cups MILK
1/8 tsp. PEPPER	1 cup LIGHT CREAM
1/8 tsp. PAPRIKA	1 cup minced boiled LOBSTER
	2 Tbsp. BUTTER

In top of a double boiler, combine tapioca, salt, pepper, paprika, onion, milk and cream. Cook 10-15 minutes over rapidly boiling water, stirring often. Add lobster and butter and mix well. Continue cooking over hot water for 15-20 minutes. Serve in soup bowls, garnished with a **thin slice of TOMATO** and sprinkled with **CHIVES** or **grated LEMON RIND**.

White Wine & Mussel Soup

6 PEPPERCORNS	1 BAY LEAF
1 cup WHITE WINE	3/4 Tbsp. THYME
1 ONION, finely chopped	3 qts. fresh MUSSELS
2 Tbsp. coarsely chopped PARSLEY	SEASONINGS of choice
	PARSLEY sprigs for garnish

In a kettle, combine peppercorns, wine, onion, parsley, bay leaf and thyme. Bring to a boil and simmer for 2 minutes. Add mussels, cover and boil, stirring occasionally, for 6 minutes, or until mussels open. With a slotted spoon, remove mussels from kettle and portion between soup bowls. Strain the cooking liquids; add seasonings to taste. Spoon or pour liquid over mussels and garnish each bowl with sprigs of parsley.

About Mussels

Fresh mussels are generally available year-round. The most abundant mussel is the blue or common mussel found along the Atlantic and Pacific coasts. Its shell is dark blue and 2 to 3 inches in length.

California Crab Gazpacho

1 cup chopped CELERY
1/2 bunch PARSLEY, chopped
1/4 cup RED WINE VINEGAR
32 oz. V-8® JUICE
1 cup chopped TOMATOES
1 cup chopped GREEN BELL
   PEPPER

3 cloves GARLIC, minced
1 CUCUMBER, chopped
1 cup CHICKEN BROTH
SALT and PEPPER to taste
JUICE of 2 LEMONS
Grated PEEL of 1 LEMON
1 lb. CRABMEAT

This soup, traditionally served chilled, may be smooth or chunky. For smooth gazpacho, blend all ingredients, except crabmeat, in a blender or food processor until smooth. Gently fold in crabmeat before serving. For chunky soup, mix together all ingredients, then gently fold in crabmeat. Chill well before serving. Garnish with **LEMON WEDGES, PARSLEY** and **CROUTONS.**

Serves 4.

Souper Grouper

1 1/2 lbs. GROUPER, TILEFISH, AMBERJACK, SHARK
   or SNAPPER FILLETS
1/2 cup chopped ONION
1/2 cup chopped GREEN BELL PEPPER
1/2 cup chopped CELERY
2 Tbsp. chopped fresh PARSLEY
4 cups WATER
SALT and PEPPER to taste
1 LEMON, thinly sliced

Cut fish fillets into 1-inch pieces. In a saucepan, cook onion, bell pepper, celery and parsley over medium-high heat for 3-4 minutes, stirring constantly. Add small amounts of water as needed to keep vegetables from burning. When vegetables are tender, add fish, salt and pepper and heat to a simmer. Add remaining water and simmer for 15 minutes. Float lemon slices in soup and serve.

Serves 4.

Creole Gumbo

This Creole dish is a favorite of New Orleans' culinary community.
"Gumbo" is a derivation of the African word for "okra."

3 slices BACON, cut in half
4 ONIONS, finely chopped
4 cloves GARLIC, finely minced
2 BAY LEAVES
2 Tbsp. finely minced GREEN BELL PEPPER
1 tsp. finely chopped fresh THYME
1 1/2 tsp. SUGAR
SALT and PEPPER to taste
2 lb. fresh OKRA, cut into 1/2-inch pieces
2 Tbsp. OIL
1 lg. HAM BONE, halved or quartered
1/2 lb. CHICKEN WINGS
1 lb. boneless VEAL STEW MEAT, cut in 1-inch cubes
1/3 cup chopped fresh PARSLEY
4 ripe TOMATOES, peeled and cored
1/2 tsp. TABASCO®
1/4 cup WORCESTERSHIRE SAUCE
JUICE of 1/2 LEMON
3 lbs. SHRIMP, peeled and deveined
2 lbs. CRABMEAT
2 cups OYSTERS with liquor
1 tsp. FILÉ POWDER
Fresh cooked RICE

Place bacon slices in a large soup kettle and cook over low heat until crispy; remove, drain on paper towels and set aside. Add onion to bacon drippings in the kettle and cook over moderate heat until golden brown, stirring constantly. Add garlic, bay leaves, bell pepper, thyme, sugar, salt and pepper and cook slowly until bell pepper is tender. Add okra to kettle and cook for 5 minutes, stirring constantly. In a large skillet, heat oil; add ham bone, chicken wings and veal cubes and cook over medium heat, stirring to brown meats on all sides. Drain any excess fat and add meats and bones to the kettle. Pour 1 cup of water into the skillet and use a wooden spoon to loosen the

(continued next page)

Creole Gumbo (continued)

browned particles that cling to the bottom and sides; stir and pour this into the kettle. Add parsley, tomatoes, Tabasco, Worcestershire sauce and lemon juice. Stir in shrimp, crab, oysters, oyster liquor and reserved bacon. Add enough water to cover all the ingredients; bring the gumbo to a boil, then turn off heat. Stir in the filé powder. Do not boil again. Remove bay leaves. Spoon cooked rice into each soup bowl, then ladle the gumbo on or around the rice.

Serves 4-6.

Caribbean Conch Chowder

2 ONIONS, chopped
1/2 cup VEGETABLE OIL
SALT and PEPPER to taste
JUICE of 3 LEMONS
2 cans (28 oz. ea.) TOMATOES, chopped
1 1/2 cups pounded and chopped CONCH
4 med. POTATOES, peeled and chunked
4 stalks CELERY, cut into bite-size pieces
4 CARROTS, cut into bite-size pieces
2 cups WATER
1/4 tsp. HOT PEPPER SAUCE
2 cups sliced OKRA
2 BAY LEAVES
1/2 tsp. PARSLEY

In a large kettle, sauté onions in oil until translucent. Add salt and pepper. Add lemon juice, tomatoes and conch and increase heat. Add vegetables and rest of ingredients. Bring to a boil, then simmer for 3 hours. Remove bay leaves and serve.

Serves 8 to 10.

About Conchs
(kongk, konch)

The beautiful, brightly colored spiral conch shell is found in southern waters and is particularly popular with Floridians and Caribbeans.

Clam & Cheddar Chowder

1 can (11 oz.) CHEDDAR CHEESE SOUP
1/2 cup MILK
1 can (8 oz.) STEWED TOMATOES, chopped, juices reserved
1 can (6 oz.) minced CLAMS, liquor reserved
2 Tbsp. DRY WHITE WINE
Dash of PEPPER
CRACKERS

In a saucepan, whisk together cheese soup and milk until well-blended. Add tomatoes and their juices, clams and liquor and wine. Season with pepper and mix well. Bring mixture to a boil. Serve with crackers on the side.

Serves 4.

Crab & Corn Chowder

1 Tbsp. MARGARINE
1 cup chopped ONION
1/3 cup chopped CELERY
1/2 cup chopped GREEN BELL PEPPER
1/2 cup chopped RED BELL PEPPER
1 Tbsp. FLOUR
1 can (14.5 oz.) CHICKEN BROTH
2 cups SKIM MILK
1 can (12 oz.) EVAPORATED SKIM MILK
8-12 oz. CRABMEAT
2 cups fresh or frozen CORN
1/2 tsp. PEPPER
1/2 tsp. PAPRIKA

In a large saucepan, melt margarine and then add onion, celery and bell pepper. Sauté, uncovered, over medium heat for 4-5 minutes or until vegetables are soft. Gradually add flour to vegetable mixture and cook for 2 minutes, stirring constantly. Slowly stir in chicken broth and bring to a boil. Add skim milk, evaporated milk, crabmeat, corn, pepper and paprika. Heat, stirring occasionally, for 5 minutes or until chowder is hot.

Serves 6.

Manhattan Clam Chowder

4 slices BACON or SALT PORK, chopped
1 med. ONION, finely chopped
2 med. POTATOES, peeled and diced
1 1/2 cups minced CLAMS, drained, liquor reserved
SALT and PEPPER to taste
2 cups TOMATO JUICE
Pinch of THYME
PAPRIKA
PARSLEY, chopped

In a skillet, fry bacon until crisp then remove to paper towels to drain. Add onions to drippings and sauté until light brown. In a saucepan, boil potatoes until just tender. Remove potatoes from pan and allow potato water to reduce by half, then add bacon, onion, reserved clam liquor and potatoes. Bring mixture to a boil and let simmer for 5 minutes. Season to taste with salt and pepper. Add tomato juice and, if soup is too thick, more of the clam liquor. Bring soup to boiling, add clams and heat through. Sprinkle with thyme. Serve soup in heated cups or bowls garnished with paprika and parsley.

Artichoke & Oyster Soup

1/2 cup chopped SHALLOTS
1 cup chopped CELERY
1/2 stick BUTTER
1 BAY LEAF
1/8 cup THYME
1 qt. CHICKEN CONSOMMÉ
20 uncooked OYSTERS
1 can (water packed) ARTICHOKE HEARTS
2 EGG YOLKS, beaten
1 cup CREAM
SALT and PEPPER to taste

In a skillet, sauté shallots and celery in butter. Stir in spices and consommé and simmer for 10 minutes. Add oysters and artichokes and simmer for an additional 15 minutes. Remove from heat and blend in egg yolks and cream. Season to taste.

New England Clam Chowder

1/4 lb. SALT PORK, 1/8-inch dice
1 cup finely chopped ONION
3 cups COLD WATER
4 cups POTATOES, 1/4-inch dice
24 shucked CLAMS, coarsely
   chopped, liquor reserved

2 cups HEAVY CREAM
1/8 tsp. THYME
SALT and PEPPER to taste
2 Tbsp. BUTTER, softened
PAPRIKA

In a heavy 2-quart saucepan, over high heat, fry salt pork, stirring constantly for about 3 minutes until a thin film of fat covers the bottom of pan. Reduce heat to moderate, stir in onions and sauté for 5 minutes. When pork and onions are light golden brown, add cold water and potatoes. Boil over high heat, then reduce heat and simmer, covered, for about 15 minutes. Add clams and their liquor, cream and thyme and heat almost to boiling. Season with salt and pepper. Stir in butter. When serving, sprinkle top with paprika.

Tuna Chowder

1 can (14.5 oz.) CHICKEN BROTH
1 can WATER
1 cup diced POTATOES
1 lb. YELLOWFIN TUNA STEAKS,
   skinned and cubed
1/2 cup chopped ONION
1/2 cup chopped CARROTS

1/2 cup chopped CELERY
1/2 cup frozen CORN
1/2 tsp. dried BASIL
1/4 tsp. dried THYME
1/2 cup MILK
1 Tbsp. chopped PARSLEY

In a large saucepan, mix broth with water. Add potatoes and simmer for 10-15 minutes or until tender. Remove potatoes from broth, reserving liquid. In a blender, purée cooked potatoes with 1/4 cup of broth. Add tuna, vegetables, seasonings and puréed potatoes to remaining broth in saucepan. Simmer for 8-10 minutes until fish flakes easily. Stir in milk and heat to serving temperature; do not boil. Sprinkle with parsley just before serving.

Serves 4.

Fish Soup with Aïoli

2 lbs. WHITEFISH STEAKS, cut into 2-inch serving pieces
COURT-BOUILLON (see p. 82)
SALT
WHITE PEPPER
LEMON JUICE

Prepare *Court-Bouillon.* Add fish, bring to a boil and simmer, uncovered, for 3-8 minutes. Transfer fish pieces to a heated serving platter as they are done. Cover loosely to keep warm. Place 1 1/3 cups *Aïoli* in a 4-quart saucepan (unheated). Add the remaining 4 egg yolks one at a time, beating with a whisk. Add 1 cup of hot *Court-Bouillon,* beating constantly, then gradually beat in all of the remaining broth. Cook over low heat, stirring until the soup coats whisk lightly. Do not boil. Season as desired. Serve with remaining *Aïoli* on the side.

Note: See Fish Substitution Chart on page 5.

Aïoli
(French Garlic Mayonnaise Sauce)

1 Tbsp. fine dry BREAD CRUMBS
1 Tbsp. WINE VINEGAR
6 cloves GARLIC, coarsely chopped
7 EGG YOLKS, reserve 4 yolks
1/2 tsp. SALT
1/8 tsp. WHITE PEPPER
1 1/2 cups OLIVE OIL
1 Tbsp. LEMON JUICE

In a bowl, soak bread crumbs in the wine vinegar for 5 minutes, then squeeze crumbs dry in a small towel. Place bread crumbs in a heavy mixing bowl, add garlic cloves and, with a wooden spoon, mash crumbs and garlic to a smooth paste. Beat in 2 egg yolks, one at a time. Beat in a third egg yolk, adding the salt and white pepper. Beat in the olive oil a few drops at a time. When mixture is as thick as cream, transfer it to a large mixing bowl. With a whisk, beat in the rest of the oil, 1 teaspoon at a time. The sauce should be the consistency of mayonnaise. Season with lemon juice.

Seafood Salads

Classic Crab Louie

1 1/2 qts. shredded SALAD GREENS
1 lb. DUNGENESS CRABMEAT

Garnish:
 1/2 lb. DUNGENESS CRAB LEGS
 2 HARD-BOILED EGGS, quartered
 2 TOMATOES, quartered
 PARSLEY SPRIGS
 LEMON WEDGES

Line salad plates or bowls with salad greens and mound with crabmeat. Pour *Green Pepper Sauce* over crabmeat. Garnish plates with crab legs, eggs, tomatoes, parsley and lemon wedges.

Serves 4.

Green Pepper Sauce

1 cup LIGHT MAYONNAISE
1/4 cup CHILI SAUCE
2 Tbsp. finely chopped GREEN BELL PEPPER
2 Tbsp. finely chopped ONION
2 Tbsp. finely chopped PARSLEY
1/4 tsp. CAYENNE

Combine all ingredients, cover and refrigerate until ready to serve.

Albacore Salad

1 lb. ALBACORE TUNA, poached
2 cans (15 oz. ea.) WHITE BEANS, drained
1/2 cup minced RED ONION
1/2 cup chopped YELLOW BELL PEPPER
1/2 cup chopped fresh PARSLEY
1/2 cup chopped oil-packed dried TOMATOES
2 cloves GARLIC, chopped
1/2 tsp. PEPPER
1/2 tsp. dry BASIL or 1 Tbsp. chopped fresh BASIL
4 Tbsp. LEMON JUICE
2 Tbsp. EXTRA-VIRGIN OLIVE OIL

In a large bowl, break tuna into bite-size pieces. Add remaining ingredients and gently toss to combine flavors. Cover and refrigerate at least 4 hours before serving.

Serves 6.

Mandarin Seafood Salad

1/2 cup MAYONNAISE
1/2 cup ORANGE JUICE
1 Tbsp. HONEY
1 Tbsp. toasted SESAME
    SEEDS
1 tsp. grated ORANGE PEEL
1/2 tsp. CURRY POWDER
6 cups torn SALAD GREENS
1/2 lb. SURIMI, flavor of choice
1 can (11 oz.) MANDARIN ORANGES, drained
1/2 cup sliced RADISHES
1/2 cup sliced WATER CHESTNUTS
1/4 cup chopped GREEN ONIONS

Combine the first 6 ingredients in a jar with a tight fitting lid. Cover and shake well until smooth and blended; refrigerate until needed. Combine remaining ingredients in a large salad bowl; add dressing and toss well. Serve immediately.

Serves 6.

Mexican Seafood Fajita Salad

2 Tbsp. VEGETABLE OIL, divided
1 Tbsp. LEMON JUICE
1 tsp. CUMIN
1/2 tsp. CHILI POWDER
1 clove GARLIC, minced
1 1/2 lbs. med. SHRIMP, peeled and deveined, or any
    firm-textured FISH (such as MULLET)*, cut into 1-inch pieces
1 lg. ONION, halved lengthwise and thinly sliced
1 lg. RED BELL PEPPER, thinly sliced
6 FLOUR TORTILLAS, warmed
6 Tbsp. SALSA, plus additional for serving
1 med. head ICEBERG LETTUCE, finely shredded
1 lg. AVOCADO, peeled and thinly sliced

In a medium bowl, combine 1 tablespoon of oil, lemon juice, cumin, chili powder and garlic and mix well. Stir in seafood and marinate for 20 minutes, stirring occasionally. In a large skillet, heat remaining oil and sauté onion and bell pepper over medium-high heat for 5 minutes or until tender but not brown. Add seafood with marinade and cook for 4 minutes; set aside. Place a tortilla on each salad plate and spread with 1 tablespoon of salsa. Divide lettuce equally over the top of each tortilla. Spoon warm seafood mixture over lettuce and garnish with avocado slices. Serve with additional salsa on the side.

Serves 6.

*See Fish Substitution Chart page 5.

 About Mullets

Striped (or Common) Mullets are firm-textured fish that possess a wholesome flesh with pronounced flavor. They thrive in shallow coastal waters and are plentiful around the Florida Keys and on the Gulf Coast.

Garden Seafood Pasta Salad

1/2 lb. fresh GREEN BEANS, snapped
1 pkg. ITALIAN SALAD DRESSING MIX
3 Tbsp. finely chopped fresh OREGANO
3 Tbsp. finely chopped fresh BASIL
1 pkg. (12 oz.) CORKSCREW PASTA,
    cooked and drained
1 pkg. (8 oz.) flake-style SURIMI,
    flavor of choice
1/3 cup sliced BLACK OLIVES
1/2 cup grated PARMESAN CHEESE
2 Tbsp. sliced GREEN ONIONS

Place green beans in a large skillet, add enough water to cover the bottom of the pan. Bring to a boil, cover and cook for 2 minutes. Drain beans in colander, rinse with cold water and set aside. Prepare salad dressing mix according to package directions; add oregano and basil and set aside. In a large bowl, combine green beans, pasta and remaining ingredients. Add dressing and toss well. Cover and refrigerate until ready to serve.

Shark Salad

2 cups cooked and flaked SHARK, TILEFISH, AMBERJACK,
    GROUPER or SNAPPER
1 cup SEEDLESS RED GRAPES, halved
1 cup chopped CELERY
1/4 cup sliced ALMONDS, toasted
1/4 tsp. SALT
1/4 tsp. CURRY POWDER
1/2 cup MAYONNAISE
LETTUCE

In a large bowl, combine all ingredients except lettuce; toss lightly. Arrange a bed of lettuce on salad plates, divide seafood between them and serve.

Serves 4.

Seafood Caesar Salad

Dressing:
  3 Tbsp. WHITE WINE VINEGAR
  1 Tbsp. WORCESTERSHIRE SAUCE
  1 1/2 tsp. DIJON MUSTARD
  3 cloves GARLIC, sliced
  1/2 cup OLIVE OIL
  2 Tbsp. SOUR CREAM
8 cups torn ROMAINE LETTUCE
1 cup CROUTONS
1/2 lb. cooked SHRIMP
6 Tbsp. grated PARMESAN CHEESE

Combine vinegar, Worcestershire sauce, mustard and garlic in a blender and process until garlic is puréed. With blender running, gradually add olive oil in a slow and steady stream. Add sour cream and blend until smooth. Transfer mixture to a covered glass or ceramic container and refrigerate. Combine lettuce and remaining ingredients in a large salad bowl, add chilled dressing and toss well. Serve immediately.

Serves 6.

Chesapeake Bay Crab Salad

1 lb. CRABMEAT
1/4 cup MAYONNAISE
1 tsp. chopped PIMENTO
2 tsp. DIJON MUSTARD
1 1/2 tsp. WORCESTERSHIRE
    SAUCE
1/2 tsp. SALT

1/4 tsp. HOT PEPPER SAUCE
JUICE of 1 LEMON
1 cup chopped CELERY
LETTUCE
1 LEMON, sliced
PAPRIKA

Place crabmeat in a large bowl. In another bowl, mix mayonnaise, pimento, mustard, Worcestershire sauce, salt, hot pepper sauce, lemon juice and celery and blend well. Pour over crabmeat and toss lightly. Serve in a bowl lined with lettuce leaves. Garnish with lemon slices and paprika.

Grilled Tuna Salad

4 (5-6 oz. ea.) TUNA STEAKS, 3/4 to 1-inch thick

Vinaigrette:
  3 Tbsp. WHITE WINE or BROTH
  3 Tbsp. OLIVE OIL
  2 Tbsp. RED WINE VINEGAR
  1/2 tsp. chopped fresh ROSEMARY or 1/4 tsp. dried
    ROSEMARY
  1/2 tsp. PEPPER
  1/8 tsp. SALT

1 clove GARLIC, minced
VEGETABLE COOKING SPRAY
6 cups packed torn SALAD GREENS
1 cup halved CHERRY TOMATOES

Place tuna steaks in a glass baking dish. Prepare vinaigrette by combining wine with the next 5 ingredients in a jar with a tight fitting lid; shake well. Pour 2 tablespoons of the vinaigrette over the fish; add garlic and turn fish to coat. Marinate for 15-30 minutes, turning once. Reserve remaining vinaigrette for salad dressing. Coat grill rack with cooking spray and heat for 1 minute. Place tuna on grill, 4-6 inches over the hot coals. Cover with lid or tent with foil. Cook, turning once, for 7 minutes or until tuna flakes easily when tested with a fork. Arrange salad greens on 4 plates. Place hot tuna on greens and add cherry tomatoes. Shake remaining vinaigrette well and drizzle over salad.

Serves 4.

About Tuna

High in protein, tuna are one of the most important food fish, living in temperate and tropical waters. They rank among the swiftest fish, capable of reaching speeds as fast as 45 mph. Unlike most fish, tuna cannot pump water over their gills and therefore must swim continuously in order to breathe.

Oregon Dungeness Crab Salad Niçoise

1 1/2 lbs. sm. RED POTATOES
2 Tbsp. SALT
1 lb. fresh GREEN BEANS
1 RED BELL PEPPER, julienne

Dressing:
   1 Tbsp. minced fresh GARLIC
   1/2 cup chopped fresh HERBS (rosemary, thyme, tarragon, and
       basil, or substitute 1/4 cup dried "herbes de Provence")
   3 Tbsp. DIJON MUSTARD
   1/2 Tbsp. crushed RED PEPPER
   4-6 ANCHOVIES, finely chopped
   1 cup EXTRA-VIRGIN OLIVE OIL
   1/2 cup fresh-squeezed LEMON JUICE
   SALT and PEPPER to taste

1 head CURLY ENDIVE, separated, washed and dried
1 head LETTUCE, separated, washed and dried
1 lb. DUNGENESS CRABMEAT
1/4 cup CAPERS
1/2 cup sliced BLACK OLIVES

Quarter potatoes, place in a large saucepan and cover with cold water. Add salt and bring potatoes to a simmer over medium heat; do not boil. Cook for 10-15 minutes or until just tender; drain and spread on a cookie sheet to dry. Blanch green beans and bell pepper quickly in boiling water, then rinse in cold tap water; drain and pat dry with paper towels. In a large bowl, combine beans and bell pepper with potatoes. In another bowl, combine dressing ingredients, gradually whisking in the olive oil until lightly emulsified. Whisk in lemon juice and adjust seasonings. Moisten the potato mixture with a small amount of dressing. Arrange a bed of curly endive and lettuce on salad plates and add a portion of the potato mixture to each. Top with crabmeat and garnish with capers and olives. Serve with remaining dressing on the side.

Serves 4.

Walnut Shrimp Salad

1 Tbsp. BUTTER
1 cup WALNUTS
1 Tbsp. SOY SAUCE
1 cup WATER CHESTNUTS
1 cup chopped CELERY
1 cup sliced GREEN ONIONS

1 cup MANDARIN ORANGES, chopped
2 lbs. cooked SHRIMP
1/2 cup SWEET AND SOUR DRESSING
LETTUCE

In a saucepan, melt butter, stir in walnuts and soy sauce, remove from heat. In a large bowl, mix water chestnuts, celery, onion, orange and shrimp. Add walnut mixture and toss with sweet and sour dressing. Arrange a bed of lettuce on salad plates and add a portion of walnut shrimp mixture to each.

Serves 6.

 Did You Know?

During the winter months, blue crabs move into deeper water and enter a state of semi-hibernation.

Crab Stuffed Avocados

1 can (6.5 oz.) CRABMEAT, drained
2 HARD-BOILED EGGS, chopped
1/4 cup PICKLE RELISH
1/3 cup SOUR CREAM
1/4 tsp. SALT
1/8 tsp. RED PEPPER SAUCE
3 ripe AVOCADOS
1/2 cup shredded SWISS CHEESE

Combine all ingredients except avocados and cheese. Cut unpeeled avocados lengthwise into halves; remove pits. Place avocados cut side up in a 9 x 9 ungreased baking dish. Fill each half with 1/3 cup crabmeat mixture; sprinkle with cheese. Bake for 20 minutes, uncovered, in a 400° oven.

Seafood Entrées

Crab Imperial

1/2 cup MILK	1/2 tsp. DRY MUSTARD
1 1/2 tsp. BUTTER	1/8 tsp. CAYENNE
1 Tbsp. FLOUR	1/4 tsp. WHITE PEPPER
1 EGG YOLK	SALT and PEPPER to taste
1 Tbsp. MAYONNAISE	1 lb. CRABMEAT, chunked
1/2 tsp. WORCESTERSHIRE SAUCE	PAPRIKA

In a saucepan, heat milk to a boil. In a skillet, melt butter, whisk in flour and milk to a smooth consistency. Blend in rest of ingredients except paprika; fold in crabmeat. Place mixture in individual ramekins and top with *Garlic Bread Crumbs.* Sprinkle with paprika and bake for 15 minutes at 350°.

Garlic Bread Crumbs

3 cloves GARLIC	2 tsp. LEMON JUICE
1/4 lb. BUTTER	1/2 tsp. PEPPER
1 1/2 cups soft BREAD CRUMBS	

Sauté garlic in butter; fold in rest of ingredients.

Dungeness Cakes Italienne

1 lb. DUNGENESS CRABMEAT
1 cup grated PARMESAN CHEESE
1 tsp. chopped fresh PARSLEY
1 clove GARLIC, minced
2 EGGS, slightly beaten
SALT and PEPPER to taste
3 Tbsp. OLIVE OIL

In a bowl, combine crabmeat, Parmesan cheese, parsley and garlic. Add eggs and mix. Form into small patties. Season with salt and pepper. Heat olive oil in a skillet and cook patties until golden brown on each side.

Serves 4.

Crab Quiche

1 (10-inch) unbaked PIE SHELL
1 cup shredded GRUYÈRE CHEESE
4 lbs. CRABMEAT
2 EGGS
1/2 cup HALF AND HALF
1/4 tsp. SALT
1/4 tsp. NUTMEG
1 tsp. chopped fresh PARSLEY

Preheat oven to 425°. Line pastry shell with foil; fill with rice, beans or metal pie weights. Bake 10 minutes; remove weights and foil from pastry shell. Reduce oven temperature to 325°. Return pastry shell to the oven; bake 10 minutes longer. Cool on a wire rack. Sprinkle half of the cheese into cooled pastry shell. Top with crabmeat. In a medium bowl, beat eggs, stir in half and half, salt, nutmeg and parsley. Pour over crabmeat; sprinkle with remaining cheese. Bake 55-65 minutes or until a knife inserted in the center comes out clean. Cool for 10 minutes before cutting.

Serves 6.

Dungeness Crab Omelet

1 Tbsp. OLIVE OIL
1 sm. ONION, minced
1 cup DUNGENESS CRABMEAT
4 EGGS, beaten
2 Tbsp. grated PARMESAN CHEESE
1 Tbsp. minced PARSLEY

In an omelet pan, heat olive oil over medium heat. Add onion and sauté until translucent. In a bowl, mix crabmeat, eggs and Parmesan cheese together and add to the sautéed onion. Reduce heat slightly. As the omelet cooks, lift with a spatula, letting the uncooked part run underneath. When the top looks creamy and almost set, increase the heat to let it brown slightly on the bottom. Slide the omelet onto a warmed plate and fold it in half. Garnish with parsley.

Crab Curry

3 Tbsp. BUTTER
2 med. ONIONS, chopped
1 lb. CRABMEAT

SALT and PEPPER to taste
Dash of CAYENNE
Cooked RICE

In a large skillet, melt butter and sauté onions. Add crabmeat, salt, pepper and cayenne and stir. Stir *Curry Sauce* into skillet and cook over low heat until crabmeat is heated through. Serve over rice.

Curry Sauce

3 Tbsp. FLOUR
2 Tbsp. BUTTER, melted
2 cups MILK

1 tsp. CURRY POWDER
2 Tbsp. WATER

In a saucepan, combine flour, butter and milk. Dissolve curry powder in water and add to flour mixture. Cook until thickened.

Serves 6.

Crabmeat Benedict

HOLLANDAISE SAUCE (see p. 88)
1 1/2 cups chopped CRABMEAT
1 tsp. BUTTER or MARGARINE
3 ENGLISH MUFFINS, halved, toasted and buttered
6 POACHED EGGS

Prepare **Hollandaise Sauce.** Heat crabmeat in butter until hot. Place a portion of crabmeat on each muffin half, add a poached egg and spoon **Hollandaise Sauce** on top.

Sautéed Abalone

4 slices ABALONE, well-pounded
1 cup + 2 Tbsp. LEMON JUICE
1/3 cup FLOUR
SALT and PEPPER to taste

1 EGG, well-beaten
1 Tbsp. BUTTER
2 Tbsp. OLIVE OIL
2 Tbsp. CAPERS

Marinate abalone in 1 cup lemon juice for 3-5 minutes. Combine flour, salt and pepper in a shallow dish. Dredge abalone in flour mixture then in egg and again in flour mixture. Over high heat, melt butter in a heavy skillet, add oil and sauté abalone for 2 1/2 minutes per side. Sprinkle with lemon juice and capers before serving.

Serves 4.

About Abalone

Sometimes called an ear shell, *the abalone feeds on the plant life that it can scrape off the rocks with its filelike tongue and can consume its weight in kelp each day. The abalone has a brick-red outer shell that occasionally has bands of green or white, surrounded by a black, hairlike fringe. The abalone's iridescent mother-of-pearl shell, which can be up to 12 inches long, is used in making costume jewelry.*

Two Ways to Cook Lobsters

The following cooking times are for hard shell lobsters; if cooking new shell lobsters, reduce cooking time by three minutes. When antennae pull out easily, the lobsters are done.

To **STEAM** lobsters, put 2 inches of seawater or salted fresh water in a large kettle with a steaming rack. Bring water to a rolling boil, then place lobsters on the rack; begin timing. Steam lobsters 13 minutes for the first pound and 3 minutes per pound for each additional pound.

To **BOIL** lobsters, fill a large kettle one-half to not more than two-thirds full of water. Bring water to a rolling boil and add lobsters, head first, to kettle. Cover kettle tightly and return to a boil. Boil lobsters 10 minutes for the first pound and 3 minutes per pound for each additional pound.

How To Eat Lobsters

Twist off the large claws and crack with a nutcracker, pliers, etc.

 Separate the tail from the body by arching the back until it cracks; break off the tail flippers.

 Insert a fork at the end of the tail and push the tail meat forward and out in one piece. Discard the black vein which runs the entire length of the tail.

 Unhinge the back shell from the body and discard the green substance *(tomalley)* you will find there.

 Open the body by cracking it apart sideways. Lobster meat lies in the joints where the small walking legs are attached.

About Lobsters

The American lobster can be found from the Canadian Maritimes down to North Carolina, but is most abundant in Maine waters. The American or Maine lobster is a crustacean with two strong claws. The clawless spiny lobster, of more southerly waters, is a distant relation of the American lobster. A spiny lobster is sometimes referred to as a crayfish, crawfish, rock lobster or langosta.

Lobster Thermidor

1 (2 lb.) LOBSTER, boiled
4 Tbsp. BUTTER, divided
2 Tbsp. FLOUR
1 cup CREAM
1/2 tsp. SALT
1/2 tsp. DRY MUSTARD
4 Tbsp. SHERRY
1 EGG YOLK
1 cup quartered fresh MUSHROOMS
1/2 cup grated PARMESAN CHEESE
PAPRIKA

Split lobster lengthwise, remove meat and cut into 1-inch cubes. Melt 2 tablespoons of butter in a skillet, add flour and cook until bubbly. Add cream, salt and mustard; cook until thick. Add sherry and egg yolk, stirring thoroughly. Keep mixture warm in top of double boiler over hot water. In a skillet, sauté mushrooms in remaining 2 tablespoons of butter and add the lobster meat. Stir, then add sherry sauce. Sprinkle part of the cheese in the bottom of the lobster shells, add lobster mixture and sprinkle cheese on top. Dust with paprika and brown in oven at 375°.

Deviled Lobster

2 cups diced LOBSTER MEAT
1 cup soft BREAD CRUMBS
1 HARD-BOILED EGG, chopped
2 tsp. LEMON JUICE
1 Tbsp. BUTTER

1 Tbsp. ANCHOVY PASTE
1 Tbsp. FLOUR
1 cup MILK
1/2 tsp. SALT

In a bowl, mix lobster with half of the bread crumbs. Add chopped egg and lemon juice and combine. In a saucepan, melt butter, blend in anchovy paste and flour, add milk and salt and cook until thickened, stirring constantly. Mix well with lobster mixture. Fill greased scallop shells, or other small baking dishes with lobster mixture. Top with remaining crumbs. Brown in a 375° oven for 15 minutes.

Serves 6.

Lobster Newburg

2 (1 lb. ea.) boiled LOBSTERS	1 cup HEAVY CREAM
2 Tbsp. BUTTER	SALT and PEPPER to taste
2 sm. ONIONS, thinly sliced	1 Tbsp. SHERRY
1 cup SEAFOOD STOCK	Fresh PARSLEY for garnish

Remove meat from tails and claws of lobsters, reserving juices; set aside. Cut carcass into small pieces. Heat butter in a large sauté pan, add onion and sauté until translucent. Add lobster carcass and reserved juices. Stir in 1 cup **Seafood Stock,** cover partially and cook over high heat for 10 minutes, stirring often. Strain liquids and measure; add additional fish stock if necessary to achieve 1 1/2 cups liquid. In a heavy saucepan, reduce liquid over high heat to 3 tablespoons. Pour in cream and stir over high heat until reduced by half. Season with salt, pepper and sherry. Slice lobster tail and arrange with claw meat on a serving platter or individual plates. Drizzle with sauce and garnish with parsley.

Seafood Stock

2 lbs. whole WHITING, HALIBUT, SOLE or FLOUNDER	6-7 sprigs fresh PARSLEY
	1 BAY LEAF
2 Tbsp. BUTTER	6-7 sprigs fresh THYME
1 sm. ONION, finely chopped	SALT and PEPPER to taste
COLD WATER	

Clean and trim fish. Cut into large chunks and rinse thoroughly under running water. In a large stockpot, melt butter and sauté onion until translucent. Add fish and enough cold water to cover all. Add spices. Bring mixture to a boil, then reduce heat to a simmer and cook, uncovered, for 20 minutes, skimming surface debris occasionally. Strain through a cheese-cloth lined strainer. May refrigerate for up to two days.

Storing Lobster

A live lobster will keep for 24 hours in a refrigerator if kept moist with wet paper or seaweed.

Lobster Bake

5 lbs. SEAWEED
4 sm. ONIONS
4 sm. RED POTATOES
4 (1 to 1 1/2 lbs. ea.) LOBSTERS
4 ears SWEET CORN, shucked except the innermost leaves
2 lbs. soft shell STEAMER CLAMS
2 lbs. MUSSELS
2 cups WATER

Place a one-inch layer of seaweed (a layer of crumpled aluminum foil to raise lobsters off the bottom of pan will do) in a 16 x 12 roasting pan. Parboil onions and potatoes. Place lobsters on seaweed and arrange the corn and onions between the lobsters and the sides of the pan. Place clams, mussels and potatoes over the lobsters, keeping top level. Layer with the balance of the seaweed and add water to the pan. Cover tightly with a lid or aluminum foil and place on the stove or a preheated grill to cook. Start timing when you first see steam. Cook, covered, for 15 minutes. Remove from heat, but do not uncover for five minutes. Serve with **CLARIFIED BUTTER, CLAM BROTH** and **COLESLAW.**

Lobsters and Their Shells

Each year, lobsters stretch and squeeze out of their old shells and leave them on the bottom of the ocean, in perfect shape, right down to the claws and feelers.

Lobster Submarine

2 cups LOBSTER MEAT
2 Tbsp. MAYONNAISE
1/4 cup finely diced RED ONION
1/4 cup finely diced CELERY
Melted BUTTER
4 SUBMARINE ROLLS

Combine lobster, mayonnaise and vegetables in a bowl and mix well. Refrigerate for 1 hour. Slice rolls in half and toast. Spread with butter and top with lobster mixture.

Honey-Broiled Sea Scallops

Lime-Honey Marinade:
3 Tbsp. LIME JUICE
1 Tbsp. VEGETABLE OIL
1 Tbsp. HONEY
1 Tbsp. SOY SAUCE
1/4 tsp. ground GINGER

1 lb. SEA SCALLOPS
2 Tbsp. SESAME SEEDS

In a medium bowl, combine lime juice, oil, honey, soy sauce and ginger. Add scallops and toss to coat. Cover and refrigerate for 1 hour, stirring occasionally. Remove scallops, reserving marinade. Thread scallops evenly on 4 skewers. Place skewers on a shallow baking pan that has been sprayed with a nonstick coating. Broil 4-6 inches from source of heat for 2-3 minutes. Turn and baste with reserved marinade and continue cooking 2-3 minutes longer or until scallops are opaque throughout. Place sesame seeds on wax paper and roll each skewer over seeds to evenly coat scallops. Serve immediately.

Serves 4.

Shrimp & Scallop Sauté

2 lbs. JUMBO SCALLOPS
2 lbs. JUMBO SHRIMP,
   peeled and deveined
3 Tbsp. OLIVE OIL
SPICES of choice

4 Tbsp. BUTTER
1/2 cup CORNSTARCH
1 cup WHITE WINE
4 cups MILK
6 cups cooked RICE

In a large skillet, sauté scallops and shrimp in olive oil, and spices of choice; set aside. Melt butter in a saucepan and gradually add cornstarch and wine, stirring constantly. Slowly add milk and continue to stir until desired consistency is reached. Add shrimp and scallops; stir to blend. Serve over rice.

Serves 4-6.

Baked Scallops

2 Tbsp. DRY WHITE WINE
1 Tbsp. fresh LEMON JUICE
1/4 tsp. SALT
1/4 tsp. WHITE PEPPER
1 lb. BAY or CALICO SCALLOPS or quartered SEA SCALLOPS
1/4 cup HEAVY CREAM
1/2 cup soft BREAD CRUMBS
2 Tbsp. melted BUTTER or MARGARINE

Mix wine, lemon juice, salt and pepper in a medium bowl. Stir in scallops. Add cream and stir. Place mixture in a shallow baking dish. Place bread crumbs in a bowl, sprinkle with butter and stir to coat. Sprinkle bread crumbs over scallop mixture. Bake at 400° until scallops are done, mixture is bubbly and crumbs are browned (approximately 15 minutes).

Serves 4.

About Scallops

Scallops swim by flapping their shells, using their powerful adductor muscle. When in danger, this muscle pulls the shell tightly closed. The smaller bay and calico scallops have a sweeter-flavored meat than the more common sea scallop.

Sea Scallop Stir Fry

1/4 cup SESAME SEED OIL
1/2 tsp. chopped GARLIC
1 tsp. fresh GINGER
1 can BABY CORN
1 bunch fresh BROCCOLI,
    cut into bite-size pieces

1/2 lb. SNOW PEAS
SOY SAUCE to taste
1 1/2 lbs. SEA SCALLOPS
Cooked WHITE or BROWN
    RICE

Heat oil in a wok. Stir in garlic and ginger. Add vegetables and soy sauce. Cook over medium heat, stirring, until vegetables are tender. Add scallops and toss until scallops turn snow white. Do not overcook. Serve over rice.

Serves 4.

Broiled Scallops

1 clove GARLIC, crushed
1/4 tsp. SALT
2 Tbsp. fresh minced PARSLEY
1 Tbsp. OLIVE or VEGETABLE OIL
1/4 cup DRY VERMOUTH
1 lb. BAY or CALICO SCALLOPS or quartered SEA SCALLOPS
1/4 Tbsp. melted BUTTER or MARGARINE
1/2 cup soft BREAD CRUMBS
PAPRIKA

Combine garlic, salt, parsley, oil and vermouth in a medium bowl. Stir in scallops. Spoon scallop mixture into 4 shells, small baking dishes or ramekins and place them on a baking sheet. Broil about 4 inches from heat for 5 minutes. In a bowl, drizzle butter over bread crumbs and stir to coat. Sprinkle bread crumbs and paprika over scallop mixture and broil until lightly browned (approximately 3 minutes).

Serves 4.

Bay Scallops
& Green Onion Butter

1 lb. BAY or CALICO SCALLOPS or quartered SEA SCALLOPS

Green Onion Butter:
   1/3 cup minced GREEN ONIONS
   1/4 cup BUTTER or MARGARINE, softened
   1/4 tsp. pressed GARLIC
   2 Tbsp. minced fresh PARSLEY
   1/4 tsp. SALT
   1/4 tsp. WHITE PEPPER

Place scallops in four individual shells, ramekins or small oven proof bowls. In a small bowl, combine green onions, butter, garlic, parsley, salt and pepper. Dot scallops with *Green Onion Butter*. Bake at 450° for 8-10 minutes.

Serves 4.

Shrimp Quiche

1 cup SHRIMP, peeled and deveined	1 1/2 cups LIGHT CREAM
1 (9-inch) unbaked PIE SHELL	1/4 tsp. SALT
1/4 cup minced ONION	Dash of PEPPER
1/4 cup minced CELERY	Dash of NUTMEG
1/4 cup minced MUSHROOMS	1 1/2 cups shredded
2 Tbsp. BUTTER or MARGARINE	CHEDDAR CHEESE
4 EGGS	Minced PARSLEY

Rinse shrimp with cold water; pat dry lightly with paper towels. Pre-bake pie shell at 450° for 7-9 minutes, until slightly browned and set aside. Sauté onion, celery and mushrooms in butter until onion is translucent; set aside. Combine eggs, cream, salt, pepper and nutmeg in a bowl or blender. Sprinkle vegetable mixture, cheese and shrimp into pastry shell. Pour egg mixture over top. Sprinkle with parsley. Bake at 325° for 40-50 minutes or until knife inserted into the center comes out clean.

Serves 4-6.

How to Devein Shrimp

Use a small sharp knife to make a shallow cut down the back (outer curved side) of shrimp. Remove shell and legs and using the knife tip, pick out the black vein on the back. Working shrimp under cold running water will help free the vein.

Pickled Shrimp

1 1/2 lbs. cooked SHRIMP,	1/2 cup VEGETABLE OIL
peeled and deveined	2 Tbsp. CAPERS
1 cup WHITE VINEGAR	2 tsp. minced GARLIC
1 cup chopped RED ONION	

Combine all ingredients in a glass or ceramic bowl, cover and refrigerate for at least 12 hours. When ready to serve, remove shrimp and onions from marinade and serve over salad greens or cooked, cooled pasta.

Shrimp Linguine

1 1/2 lbs. cooked SHRIMP, peeled and deveined
1 pkg. (16 oz.) LINGUINE
6 Tbsp. BUTTER
1 Tbsp. finely chopped GARLIC
1 cup HEAVY CREAM
1/2 cup finely chopped fresh PARSLEY
3 Tbsp. finely chopped fresh BASIL or 1 tsp. dried BASIL
1/2 tsp. dried THYME
3/4 cup grated PARMESAN CHEESE
SALT and PEPPER to taste

Rinse shrimp in cold water; pat dry with paper towels. Cook linguine according to package directions until al dente. While linguine is cooking, melt butter in a large skillet. Add garlic and sauté briefly. Add cream and heat just to boiling, stirring frequently. Lower heat and stir in shrimp, parsley, basil and thyme. Continue to cook until shrimp are just heated through. Do not overcook. Remove from heat and add linguine. Toss lightly. Add Parmesan cheese, salt and pepper and toss again.

Serves 6.

Shrimp Stroganoff

1/4 cup minced ONION
1/4 cup + 1 Tbsp. BUTTER
1 1/2 lbs. SHRIMP, peeled
   and deveined
1/2 lb. MUSHROOMS, sliced

1 Tbsp. FLOUR
1 1/2 cups SOUR CREAM,
   at room temperature
SALT and PEPPER to taste
Cooked NOODLES or RICE

In a large skillet, sauté onion in 1/4 cup of butter until translucent. Add shrimp and sauté for 3-5 minutes or until pink and opaque. Transfer mixture to a casserole dish and keep warm. Heat remaining butter in the skillet, add mushrooms and sauté over medium heat until browned. Gradually add flour and stir for 2-3 minutes. Reduce heat and stir in shrimp mixture, sour cream, salt and pepper. Heat thoroughly, but do not boil. Serve over hot noodles or rice.

Shrimp Scampi

1 tsp. BUTTER	JUICE of 1 LEMON
2 tsp. OLIVE OIL	SALT and PEPPER to taste
3 cloves GARLIC, minced	Cooked NOODLES or RICE
1 lb. SHRIMP	1/4 cup finely chopped PARSLEY
1/4 cup WHITE WINE	LEMON WEDGES for garnish

In a sauté pan, melt butter and then add oil and garlic. Sauté for 1 minute. Add shrimp and sauté for 1 minute. Add wine, lemon juice, salt and pepper. Sauté quickly while sauce reduces and shrimp turns pink; do not overcook. Add noodles to serving plates, top with shrimp and drizzle with sauce. Sprinkle each with parsley and garnish with lemon wedges.

Serves 6.

Shrimp & Feta Sandwich

3/4 lb. cooked SHRIMP, peeled and deveined

Vinaigrette:

4 tsp. OLIVE OIL	1/4 tsp. dried OREGANO
3 Tbsp. LEMON JUICE	1/2 tsp. dried BASIL
2 tsp. minced GARLIC	1/8-1/4 tsp. PEPPER

1 (12 oz.) SOURDOUGH BAGUETTE
1/3 cup crumbled FETA CHEESE
1 sm. CUCUMBER, thinly sliced
1 TOMATO, sliced

Rinse shrimp with cold water; pat dry lightly with paper towels. In a small bowl, combine all vinaigrette ingredients; set aside. Cut baguette into fourths, slice in half lengthwise. Brush bottoms of each sandwich with 2 teaspoons of vinaigrette. Divide cheese equally on sandwich tops. Broil both halves just until cheese on top halves melts. Arrange cucumber and tomato slices on sandwich bottoms. Divide shrimp equally among the four sandwiches and drizzle with remaining vinaigrette. Top with melted cheese halves.

Serves 4.

Surf 'n' Turf Kabob

1/2 lb. SHRIMP, peeled
1 lb. BEEF SIRLOIN STEAK, cut into 1-inch pieces
2 ZUCCHINIS, cut diagonally into 1-inch pieces
2 EARS CORN, cut into 1-inch pieces
2 small ONIONS, cut into wedges
1 GREEN BELL PEPPER, chunked
Cooked RICE

Alternate all ingredients on skewers and grill or broil until meat reaches desired doneness. Turn kabobs often, brushing with *Lemon Basting Sauce.* Serve with rice.

Lemon Basting Sauce

1/4 cup WATER
1/2 cup KETCHUP
1/4 cup finely chopped ONION
1 Tbsp. BROWN SUGAR
3 Tbsp. LEMON JUICE

2 Tbsp. COOKING OIL
2 tsp. MUSTARD
2 tsp. WORCESTERSHIRE
   SAUCE
1/2 tsp. CHILI POWDER

In a small saucepan, combine all sauce ingredients and simmer, uncovered, for 10 minutes stirring occasionally.

Corn & Shrimp on Toast

1 can (10.75 oz.) CREAM OF MUSHROOM SOUP
1/2 cup MILK
1 tsp. PAPRIKA
1 can (4.2 oz.) TINY SHRIMP, drained
1 can (11 oz.) CORN
PEPPER to taste
TOAST POINTS

In a saucepan, combine soup, milk and paprika. Stir over low heat until mixture is smooth and evenly pink. Add shrimp, corn and pepper. Cover and cook until heated through. Serve over toast points.

Serves 4.

Sweet & Sour Shrimp

Sweet and Sour Sauce:
  2 lg. NECTARINES, pitted, do not peel
  3 lg. PLUMS, pitted, do not peel
  3 Tbsp. APRICOT PRESERVES
  5 Tbsp. DIJON MUSTARD
  1/4 tsp. dried CHILE FLAKES (or finely
    chopped JALAPEÑO PEPPER)
  SALT and PEPPER to taste
  JUICE of 1 LEMON

1 lb. cooked SHRIMP, peeled and deveined

In a blender, combine all ingredients for the sauce and purée. Fold in shrimp. Serve hot over rice or cold as an appetizer.

Serves 4.

Scallop & Shrimp Kabobs

**1/2 lb. SEA SCALLOPS (or other
    meat-like textured fish—see p. 5)**
3/4 lb. SHRIMP (tails on)
30 chunks CANTALOUPE
30 chunks HONEYDEW MELON
30 MUSHROOM CAPS
1/4 cup LEMON JUICE
2 Tbsp. BUTTER, melted

Alternate seafood, melon and mushrooms on 6 (8-inch) skewers. Combine lemon juice and butter. Broil kabobs 10 minutes, turning and brushing with lemon juice mixture until seafood is opaque. Drizzle *Brie Baste* over kabobs and broil for 1-2 minutes or until golden brown.

Brie Baste

1/4 cup BRIE CHEESE   **1/4 cup LIGHT CREAM**

In a small saucepan, melt Brie cheese and gradually whisk in cream.

Chili-Seared
Rock Shrimp Curry

2 oz. SALAD OIL
1 lb. ROCK SHRIMP
FLOUR
2 Tbsp. ASIAN CHILI PASTE
1 Tbsp. CURRY POWDER
4 Tbsp. CHICKEN STOCK
4 Tbsp. CREAM

2 cups cooked RICE
6 oz. VEGETABLES of choice,
 julienne
CILANTRO SPRIGS
4 Tbsp. finely minced BELL
 PEPPER

In a skillet, heat oil until very hot. Lightly dust shrimp in flour. Place shrimp in skillet and sauté for 30 seconds. Add chili paste and continue sautéing for another 30 seconds. Add curry powder and toss shrimp well. Add stock and cream and simmer for one minute. Divide the rice between two serving plates and top with shrimp mixture. Garnish with vegetables and cilantro sprigs; sprinkle top with peppers.

Serves 2.

Shrimp & Artichoke Bake

1/2 lb. MUSHROOMS, sliced thick
1/4 cup OLIVE OIL
2 lbs. cooked SHRIMP, peeled and deveined
1 can (14 oz.) ARTICHOKE HEARTS, cut into halves
1 1/2 cups MEDIUM WHITE SAUCE (see p. 84)
1/2 cup SHERRY
1 1/4 Tbsp. WORCESTERSHIRE SAUCE
1/2 cup grated PARMESAN CHEESE
PAPRIKA to taste
SALT and PEPPER to taste
Cooked RICE

In a skillet, sauté mushrooms in oil. Arrange shrimp in a casserole dish. Add mushrooms and artichoke hearts. Combine white sauce, sherry and Worcestershire in a bowl. Pour over shrimp and sprinkle with Parmesan, paprika, salt and pepper. Bake at 375° for 30 minutes. Serve with rice.

Serves 4.

Oyster Dressing

2 lg. stalks CELERY, chopped
1 med. ONION, chopped
1/2 cup MARGARINE or BUTTER
1 tsp. SALT
1/2 tsp. LEMON PEPPER
1/8 tsp. MACE
1/8 tsp. TARRAGON
1/8 tsp. POULTRY SEASONING
1/2 tsp. LEMON JUICE
1 pt. shucked OYSTERS, with liquor
8 slices day-old BREAD, cubed

Finely chop celery and onions. Sauté in margarine until tender. Mix in seasonings. Add oysters with liquor and simmer until edges of oysters begin to curl. Remove from heat and gently mix in bread cubes. Adjust moistness as desired.

Makes 4 cups.

Southern Scalded Oysters with Vinegar Sauce

Vinegar Sauce:
  1 cup WHITE VINEGAR
  1 sm. ONION, very thinly sliced
  SALT to taste
  Coarse ground PEPPER to taste

6 OYSTERS, in the shell

In a glass bowl, combine vinegar, onion, salt and pepper. Let stand for several hours at room temperature to blend flavors. Scrub oysters thoroughly under cool water. Place oysters in a wire basket; lower basket into rapidly boiling water to cover; cook just until shells open. Serve immediately with vinegar sauce on the side.

Serves 1. Increase all ingredients for each additional serving.

Scalloped Oysters

12-18 OYSTERS, liquor reserved   1 tsp. SALT
1/2-3/4 cup HALF AND HALF   1/4 tsp. PEPPER
3 cups soft BREAD CRUMBS   PAPRIKA
1/2 cup BUTTER, melted

Arrange oysters with liquor in a greased 12 x 7 baking dish. Pour 1/2 of the half and half over oysters. Mix remaining ingredients and sprinkle over oysters. Top with remaining half and half and sprinkle with paprika. Cook, uncovered, at 375° for 30-40 minutes.

Serves 2.

Buying Oysters

When purchasing live oysters, choose only those that close their shells tightly when handled. Live oysters should be refrigerated and kept for no more than three days. Do not store live oysters in an airtight container. Shucked oysters in their liquor should be refrigerated and used within two days.

Oyster Casserole

1 pint OYSTERS, liquor reserved   1/2 cup MILK
2 tsp. + 1/2 cup BUTTER   1 cup cooked HAM, diced
1 med. ONION, chopped   1 cup GREEN PEAS
1/2 cup diced GREEN BELL PEPPER   1 cup diced cooked
1/2 cup FLOUR   CARROTS
1/2 cup WHITE WINE

Drain oysters, reserving 1/2 cup liquor. In a skillet, add 2 teaspoons butter, onion and bell pepper; sauté vegetables until tender. In a saucepan, melt 1/2 cup butter and stir in flour. Cook 2-3 minutes until thickened. Add reserved oyster liquor, wine and milk. Cook until thickened; remove from heat and add oysters, ham, peas and vegetables. Place mixture in a 13 x 9 casserole dish and bake at 375° for 15 minutes.

Clams, Chile Pepper & Pasta

36 LITTLENECK or CHERRYSTONE CLAMS
1/4 cup VINEGAR
8 oz. GREEN LINGUINE or other PASTA
2 Tbsp. OLIVE OIL
2 Tbsp. BUTTER
1 clove GARLIC, minced
1 HOT RED CHILE PEPPER, minced
2 lg. RED BELL PEPPERS, seeded and diced
1/2 tsp. chopped fresh ROSEMARY
1/2 tsp. chopped fresh THYME LEAVES
SALT and PEPPER to taste

Scrub clams and place in a shallow baking dish. Add a mixture of the vinegar and enough water to cover. Let stand for 30 minutes, drain and rinse. Prepare pasta according to package directions; drain. Heat oil and butter in a skillet; add garlic and hot pepper. Sauté gently for 1 minute. Stir in remaining ingredients and then add clams. Cover and simmer for 4 minutes or until clams open. Serve over linguine.

Herbed Mahi Mahi

2 lbs. MAHI MAHI FILLETS, cut to serving size
1 tsp. PEPPER
1/2 cup BUTTER
1 cup thinly sliced GREEN ONIONS
1 lb. MUSHROOMS, sliced
1/4 cup fresh DILL, minced

Preheat oven to 400°. Place fillets in a buttered baking pan, sprinkle with pepper and dot with 2 tablespoons of butter. In a skillet, melt 3 tablespoons of butter, add onions and sauté for 1 minute. Add remaining butter and mushrooms and continue to cook until mushrooms have absorbed all the butter. Add dill, stir and then pour mixture over fish. Bake for 20 minutes, basting occasionally.

Serves 4-6.

Salmon with Ginger Salsa

Ginger Salsa:
  2 PEACHES or MANGOES, diced
  1 lg. TOMATO, diced, no juice
  4 GREEN ONIONS, chopped
  2 Tbsp. chopped fresh CILANTRO
  2 tsp. finely minced fresh GINGERROOT or 1/2 tsp.
      ground GINGER
  1 Tbsp. BALSAMIC VINEGAR
VEGETABLE OIL COOKING SPRAY
JUICE of 1 LEMON
4 (6 oz. ea.) SALMON STEAKS

In a bowl, combine the first six ingredients together. Heat grill and spray with vegetable oil spray. Sprinkle lemon juice over salmon. Grill salmon steaks 5-6 minutes on each side. Remove salmon from grill and place on serving plates. Top each with a portion of the salsa.

Serves 4.

Salmon Croquettes

1 can (14.75 oz.) PINK SALMON, drained
1 1/2 cups thick WHITE SAUCE (see p. 84)
1 Tbsp. LEMON JUICE
1 EGG, beaten
1 cup fine BREAD CRUMBS

Remove skin and bones from salmon and discard; flake salmon and place in a bowl. Add 1 cup white sauce and lemon juice and mix thoroughly. Cool and shape into croquettes, roll in egg to coat, then in bread crumbs. Wrap in plastic wrap and freeze. Remove from freezer; thaw for 5-10 minutes at room temperature. Fry in deep oil heated to 375° until golden brown. Serve with remaining white sauce drizzled over tops.

Serves 8.

Note: Croquettes may be shaped into small cylinders, ovals or rounds.

Smoked Salmon Cheesecake

1/2 cup crushed CRACKERS
2 pkgs. (8 oz. ea.) CREAM CHEESE, softened
4 EGGS
1 cup MONTEREY JACK CHEESE, shredded
1/2 cup SOUR CREAM
4 oz. SMOKED SALMON, chopped
1/4 cup minced RED ONION
1/4 cup chopped RED BELL PEPPER
1/4 cup chopped GREEN BELL PEPPER
1 tsp. dried DILL
1/4 tsp. CAYENNE

Sprinkle cracker crumbs in the bottom of a lightly greased 9-inch springform pan; set aside. In mixer bowl, beat cream cheese on medium speed until fluffy. Add eggs, one at a time, beating well after each addition. Add remaining ingredients and mix until well-blended. Pour into prepared pan. Bake at 325° for 45-50 minutes. Cool on a wire rack for 10 minutes. Gently run a knife around the edge of the pan to release sides. Cool completely. Refrigerate until serving time. Serve at room temperature with crackers.

Makes 25 servings.

About Salmon

Ninety percent of all North American salmon are found off the Pacific coast and come from Alaskan waters. Salmon varieties include: chinook or king salmon, coho or silver salmon, sockeye or red salmon, pink or humpback salmon and chum or dog salmon. Atlantic salmon is provided mostly by Canadian sources. Salmon are born in a fresh-water stream and most spend their life in the ocean. They then return to the same stream to reproduce, sometimes swimming 2,000 miles upstream to the same spot at which they were born.

King Salmon Quiche

3 lg. POTATOES, thinly sliced
1 (9-inch) PIE SHELL
1 cup KING SALMON,
   cooked and flaked
2 EGGS

1/2 cup MILK
1 cup COTTAGE CHEESE
1 Tbsp. chopped fresh DILL
1/4 tsp. SALT
1/4 tsp. PEPPER

Layer potato slices in pie crust, then add flaked salmon. Mix remaining ingredients in mixing bowl and pour carefully over pie. Bake at 325° for 25-30 minutes or until knife inserted in center comes out clean. Serve at room temperature or chilled.

Serves 6.

Did You Know?

Many scientists believe salmon are able to return to their spawning grounds by somehow sensing ocean currents, the earth's magnetic field and by following the scent emitted from those spawning grounds.

Salmon Loaf

1 can (14.75 oz.) SALMON,
   juice reserved
1/3 cup HOT MILK
1 cup soft BREAD CRUMBS
1 tsp. minced ONION
1 tsp. LEMON JUICE

Dash of CAYENNE
1/2 tsp. NUTMEG
1 Tbsp. chopped PARSLEY
SALT to taste
2-3 EGGS, separated

Remove skin and bones from salmon and discard. Flake salmon. Combine milk and bread crumbs. Add onion, lemon juice, seasonings, salmon juice and egg yolks. Fold in stiffly beaten egg whites. Pour into a greased baking dish. Bake at 350° for 45 minutes or until firm in the center and delicately browned.

Serves 8.

Cucumber-Yogurt Salmon

4 (4-6 oz.) SALMON FILLETS
1 tsp. SALT
WATER
1 med. CUCUMBER, peeled, seeded and thinly sliced
1 cup chopped TOMATOES
1 cup PLAIN YOGURT
SALT and PEPPER to taste
2 Tbsp. chopped fresh DILL

Preheat oven to 425°. Arrange salmon fillets on 4 pieces of foil that measure 15 x 12. Bring salted water to boil in a saucepan, add cucumber slices and return to a boil over high heat. Cook for 30 seconds. Drain and rinse under cold running water; drain and pat dry. Spread 1/4 cup of yogurt over each piece of salmon. Top with cucumber slices and tomato. Season with salt and pepper and sprinkle with dill. Fold top of foil over bottom and crimp edges tightly to seal. Arrange packets in a single layer on a baking sheet. Bake 10-12 minutes, until foil is puffed and fish is cooked through.

Serves 4.

Grilled Salmon

Lemon-Dill Marinade:
   3 Tbsp. OLIVE OIL
   3 Tbsp. LEMON JUICE
   3 Tbsp. SOY SAUCE
   2 tsp. chopped fresh DILL
   1/4 tsp. SALT

4 SALMON STEAKS
LEMON WEDGES

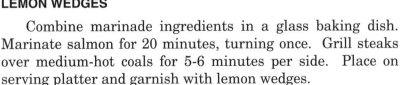

Combine marinade ingredients in a glass baking dish. Marinate salmon for 20 minutes, turning once. Grill steaks over medium-hot coals for 5-6 minutes per side. Place on serving platter and garnish with lemon wedges.

Serves 4.

Pan-Seared Alaska Salmon

4 (6-8 oz. ea.) ALASKA SALMON FILLETS or STEAKS
SALT and PEPPER to taste
1 Tbsp. OLIVE OIL
4 tsp. chopped fresh CILANTRO

Preheat oven to 400°. Lightly season salmon with salt and pepper. Heat an oven-proof sauté pan over medium heat for 2 minutes; add olive oil. Sear salmon on one side for 2-3 minutes. Turn salmon over and place the entire pan in the oven. Bake for 4-8 minutes, or until fish flakes easily when tested with a fork. To serve, make a 1-ounce pool of the *Orange Vinaigrette Sauce* in the center of 4 serving plates. Top with salmon and garnish with cilantro.

Orange Vinaigrette Sauce

1 cup ORANGE JUICE
1 1/2 Tbsp. minced RED ONION
1 1/2 Tbsp. LIME JUICE
1 tsp. HONEY-DIJON MUSTARD
1 tsp. CHILI POWDER
1/2 cup ITALIAN SALAD DRESSING

In a small saucepan, cook orange juice over medium-high heat until reduced to the consistency of syrup; let cool slightly. Place onion, lime juice, mustard and chili powder in a blender; add cooled orange syrup. Blend for 30 seconds. With blender running, slowly drizzle in the salad dressing so that the mixture emulsifies.

Serves 4.

About Alaska Salmon

There are five species of Alaska Salmon: Chinook (King), Keta or Chum (Dog), Coho (Silver), Pink (Humpback) and Sockeye (Red). The Chinook is Alaska's state fish.

Seafood Jambalaya

1 Tbsp. VEGETABLE OIL
1 cup chopped GREEN BELL PEPPER
1 cup chopped ONION
1/2 cup thinly sliced CELERY
1 clove GARLIC, minced
1 1/4 cups uncooked LONG GRAIN RICE
1 can (14.75 oz.) TOMATOES, undrained
1 can (14.5 oz.) CHICKEN BROTH
1 cup WATER
3/4 tsp. OREGANO
1/2 tsp. THYME
1/4 tsp. CAYENNE
1/8 tsp. ALLSPICE
1 lb. CRABMEAT
2 Tbsp. LEMON JUICE

In a large saucepan, heat oil, add bell pepper, onion, celery and garlic. Cook, stirring frequently, for 4-5 minutes or until onion is soft. Add rice, cook and stir for 2 minutes. Add tomatoes, chicken broth, water and spices. Bring to a boil, reduce heat and simmer, covered, for 20 minutes. Add crabmeat and lemon juice, cook for 5-7 minutes or until rice is tender.

Serves 6.

Tuna Cashew Casserole

1 can (6 oz.) CHOW MEIN NOODLES
1 can (10.75 oz.) CREAM OF
    MUSHROOM SOUP
1/2 cup WATER
1 can (6 oz.) TUNA, drained
1/2 cup chopped CASHEWS
1 cup finely diced CELERY
1/4 cup minced ONION
SALT and PEPPER to taste

Preheat oven to 325°. Reserve 1/2 cup of noodles. Combine soup and water, add remaining noodles and the rest of the ingredients. Season to taste. Pour mixture into a 1 1/2-quart casserole dish, sprinkle top with reserved noodles. Bake, uncovered, for 25-30 minutes.

Serves 6.

Barbecued Tuna
with Lemon-Butter Baste

6 slices BACON
6 (1/2 lb. ea.) TUNA STEAKS, skin removed

Lemon-Butter Baste:
    1/2 cup BUTTER or MARGARINE
    1/4 cup LEMON JUICE
    1 med. clove GARLIC, minced or pressed
    2 Tbsp. chopped fresh PARSLEY (or 2 tsp. dried)

Wrap 1 strip of bacon around each steak and secure with a toothpick. Melt butter, stir in lemon juice, garlic and parsley; set aside. Preheat grill. Grease rack and place steaks 6 inches above the coals. Brush with lemon butter mixture several times while cooking. Allow 5 minutes per side for a 1-inch steak.

Holy Mackerel!

The phrase "Holy Mackerel" emerged in 17th century England when merchants were permitted to sell their mackerel (which spoiled easily) on Sundays despite laws prohibiting such sales.

Grilled Mackerel
with Lemon-Garlic Basting Sauce

3 lbs. dressed MACKEREL

Lemon-Garlic Basting Sauce:
    1/2 cup LEMON JUICE   **1 tsp. dried OREGANO**
    1/4 cup OLIVE OIL   **LEAVES, crushed**
    1 tsp. SALT   **1/2 tsp. PEPPER**
    3/4 tsp. GARLIC SALT

Make 4-5 shallow slits on both sides of each mackerel. Combine sauce ingredients. Brush fish inside and out with sauce. Place fish on a greased wire rack about 4 inches from medium-hot coals. Let cook for 6-8 minutes. Baste, then turn and cook for 6-8 minutes longer, basting often.

Flounder Fillets Dijon

4 lg. CARROTS, julienne	4 (4-5 oz.) FLOUNDER FILLETS
2 Tbsp. minced PARSLEY	1 tsp. coarse-grain DIJON
1 tsp. OLIVE OIL	MUSTARD
SALT and PEPPER to taste	1 tsp. HONEY

In a 2-quart microwave-safe baking dish, combine carrots, parsley, oil, salt and pepper. Cover with waxed paper. Microwave on High for 5 minutes, stirring once. Fold or bend fillets and arrange on top of carrots with the thick parts toward the outside. Combine mustard and honey and spread over the fillets. Cover with waxed paper. Microwave on High for 2 minutes. Turn fillets, placing thick parts toward the center and continue to cook for 1-3 minutes or just until fish flakes easily. Allow to stand, covered, for 2 minutes.

Serves 4.

Swordfish
with Anchovy-Butter Sauce

2 lbs. (1-inch thick) SWORDFISH STEAKS

Marinade:

1/4 cup OLIVE OIL	1 clove GARLIC
1/4 cup LEMON JUICE	1 tsp. ITALIAN SEASONING

Place swordfish steaks in a non-metallic dish. Combine marinade ingredients, pour over fish and marinate for 1 hour. Grill or broil steaks 5 minutes per side, turning once and basting frequently with marinade. Serve with warm *Anchovy-Butter Sauce* on the side.

Anchovy-Butter Sauce

1/2 cup BUTTER	1 tsp. chopped fresh
6 ANCHOVY FILLETS, mashed	PARSLEY
1/2 tsp. LEMON JUICE	

In a saucepan, melt butter, add and combine remaining ingredients. Keep warm until ready to serve.

Curried Halibut

1 cup FLOUR	1/3 tsp. LEMON PEPPER
1 1/2 tsp. minced GARLIC	1 bottle (8 oz.) FLAT BEER
1 1/2 tsp. CURRY POWDER	1 lb. HALIBUT, cubed
1 tsp. MARJORAM	2 cups PANKO
2 tsp. BAKING POWDER	(Japanese potato flakes)

In a large bowl, combine flour, garlic, curry powder, marjoram, baking powder and lemon pepper; mix well. Slowly stir in enough beer to make a thick batter. Dip halibut in batter and then roll in panko. Let stand for 2 minutes. Deep fry in 375° oil until golden brown. Drain on paper towels and serve with a tartar sauce or zesty tomato horseradish sauce for dipping.

Serves 4.

Creole Halibut

MARGARINE
2 lbs. HALIBUT, cubed

Lightly grease a 9-inch baking dish with margarine. Place halibut in baking dish, cover and bake at 350° for 20 minutes or until fish flakes easily with a fork. Place fish on a serving platter or individual plates and top with *Creole Sauce.*

Creole Sauce

1/2 cup chopped ONION	1 BAY LEAF
1 clove GARLIC, minced	4 TOMATOES, chopped
3 Tbsp. COOKING OIL	1 tsp. SALT
1/2 cup chopped GREEN BELL	1/8 tsp. PEPPER
PEPPER	TABASCO® to taste

Sauté onion and garlic in cooking oil until light brown. Add bell pepper, bay leaf, tomatoes, salt and pepper. Simmer, uncovered, for 20 minutes. Remove bay leaf and stir in Tabasco to taste.

Serves 4.

Flounder & Fennel Bake

2 FENNEL BULBS	1 Tbsp. fresh THYME
2 Tbsp. unsalted BUTTER	4 FLOUNDER FILLETS
1/4 tsp. SALT	2 med. TOMATOES, peeled,
1/8 tsp. PEPPER	chopped

Preheat oven to 425°. Trim greens off fennel bulbs and cut in half lengthwise; remove tough inner core. Cut into thin slices. In a large saucepan, melt butter over medium heat. Add fennel, salt, pepper and thyme. Reduce heat to low, cover and cook for 5-7 minutes or until tender, stirring occasionally. Butter 4 pieces of foil that measure 12 x 15. On the bottom half of each piece, place 1/4 of the fennel mixture. Lay fish over top and sprinkle with 1/4 of the chopped tomatoes. Fold over top part of the foil and crimp edges together tightly to seal. Arrange packets in a single layer on a baking sheet. Bake for 10-12 minutes, until foil is puffed and fish is cooked through.

Serves 4.

Seafood Turnovers

1/2 lb. CRABMEAT
1 pkg. (10 oz.) frozen chopped SPINACH, thawed and
   well-drained
1 cup shredded MOZZARELLA CHEESE
1/2 tsp. dried OREGANO
1/2 tsp. dried BASIL
1/2 tsp. GARLIC POWDER
2 cans (10 oz. ea.) refrigerated PIZZA DOUGH

Combine crabmeat, spinach, cheese, herbs and garlic powder; mix well. Unroll pizza dough and pat into two 14 x 11 rectangles. Cut each into 4 squares. Spoon 1/2 cup seafood mixture onto center of each square. Fold dough in half diagonally; press edges to seal well. Place on a lightly greased baking sheet and bake at 425° for 8-10 minutes or until crust is browned.

Makes 8 turnovers.

Baked Haddock

1 1/2 cups dry BREAD CRUMBS
1/2 tsp. dried DILL
3 Tbsp. SALAD OIL
1 1/2 lbs. HADDOCK FILLETS

In a large shallow dish, combine bread crumbs and dill. Pour salad oil into another shallow dish. Rinse fish, pat dry and then cut crosswise into 2-inch strips. Roll fish in oil then dredge in crumb mixture to coat. Arrange fish on a baking sheet and bake in a 400° oven for about 10 minutes or until fish flakes and looks opaque when tested in the thickest portion.

Serves 4.

 About Haddock

The dark line and black patch on the haddock's shoulder is known as "Devil's Thumbprint" or "St. Peter's Mark." Haddock meat is light textured and lean.

Beach Barbecue Bundles

4 med. POTATOES, cooked, peeled and sliced
2 med. ONIONS, sliced
1 ROCKFISH
SALT and PEPPER to taste
4 tsp. OLIVE OIL
4 cloves GARLIC, minced
2 Tbsp. LEMON JUICE
Fresh herb sprigs: PARSLEY, DILL, TARRAGON or BASIL

Layer 2 squares of foil per bundle. Brush top of foil with oil. Make one layer each of potato, onion, then fish in that order. Sprinkle salt and pepper on the top. Combine olive oil, garlic and lemon juice and pour over fish. Add herb sprigs, then fold foil over to create a tight bundle. Oven-bake bundles at 250° for 20-25 minutes, cook on a barbecue grill or in a beach barbecue pit.

Serves 4.

Pacific Red Snapper Veracruz

1 lb. PACIFIC RED SNAPPER FILLETS	1 BAY LEAF
2 Tbsp. OLIVE OIL	1/4 tsp. SALT
1 sm. ONION, thinly sliced	1/4 tsp. PEPPER
1 BELL PEPPER, thinly sliced	1 cup diced TOMATOES
3 cloves GARLIC, minced	JUICE of 2 LEMONS
1 tsp. JALAPEÑO or SERRANO CHILE, chopped	1 LEMON, sliced
1/2 tsp. OREGANO	1 AVOCADO, sliced
	Fresh CILANTRO SPRIGS

Place fish fillets in a shallow baking dish. Heat olive oil in a small skillet and sauté onion, bell pepper and garlic until vegetables are limp. Add jalapeño, oregano, bay leaf, salt, pepper, tomatoes and lemon juice. Pour mixture over fish and arrange lemon slices on top. Cover tightly and bake at 325° for 25-30 minutes or just until fish turns opaque in the center and begins to flake. During the last 5 minutes of baking, check for doneness and add liquid if needed. Continue to bake uncovered until fish is done. Garnish with avocado slices and cilantro sprigs.

Serves 4.

Swordfish Piccata

1/2 tsp. PEPPER	2 Tbsp. LEMON JUICE
1 lb. SWORDFISH CUTLETS, 1/2-inch thick	2 tsp. CAPERS
1 Tbsp. finely chopped PARSLEY	LEMON ROUNDS

Pepper swordfish cutlets and place in a broiling pan. Broil fish for 2 1/2 minutes on each side or until flesh turns opaque. Remove swordfish from pan and place on a heated serving platter. Sprinkle with parsley, lemon juice and capers. Garnish with lemon rounds.

Serves 2.

Grilled Seafood Taquitos with Corn Salsa

1 lb. ROCKFISH FILLETS
JUICE of 2 LIMES
2 tsp. OLIVE OIL
8 CORN TORTILLAS

Toppings:
LETTUCE LEAVES   LIME WEDGES
SHREDDED CABBAGE   CILANTRO SPRIGS

Prepare **Corn Salsa.** Marinate fillets in lime juice and olive oil for 1/2 hour. Grill fish until just done. Heat tortillas until pliable. With two tortillas halfway overlapping each other, place fish in center and add toppings to taste. Roll and use toothpicks to hold together or roll in waxed paper. Serve taquitos with **Corn Salsa** on the side.

Serves 4.

Corn Salsa

1 cup cooked CORN   1/2 bunch fresh CILANTRO,
1 med. RED ONION, chopped   chopped
1 cup chopped CUCUMBER   SALT and PEPPER
2 JALAPEÑO PEPPERS, minced   JUICE of 2 LIMES

Combine all salsa ingredients together and let set for 1 hour to allow flavors to blend.

About Rockfish

There are over 50 varieties of rockfish including yellowtail, blue rockfish, goldeneye, bocaccio, chilipepper, shortbelly, rock cod and Pacific red snapper. Some varieties of rockfish are referred to as ocean perch in the marketplace. Rockfish is usually sold in whole fillets and when purchased should be glistening and have no signs of browning or drying.

White Seabass
à la Niçoise

2 (8 oz. ea.) WHITE SEABASS
    FILLETS
3 PEPPERCORNS
1/2 BAY LEAF
1/2 tsp. minced ONION
1/4 tsp. dried PARSLEY
1/4 cup WHITE WINE
1 med. head BUTTER
    LETTUCE
1 lg. TOMATO, sliced
2 slices RED ONION

12 fresh whole GREEN BEANS,
    cooked
3 med. RED POTATOES, boiled
    and halved
2 flat ANCHOVY FILLETS
1 HARD-BOILED EGG,
    quartered
1 Tbsp. CAPERS
6 BLACK OLIVES
2 Tbsp. chopped fresh
    PARSLEY

Place fish fillets in liquid (water or stock) seasoned with peppercorns, bay leaf, onion, dried parsley and wine. Simmer over medium heat for 10 minutes per inch of thickness. Line a serving platter with the large outer leaves of the lettuce. Chop the remainder of the lettuce and arrange on the platter. Arrange tomato slices on one end of the platter, followed by onion slices separated into rings, green beans and potatoes. Place the poached seabass fillet in the center of the platter and top with a crisscross of anchovy. Garnish the platter with egg quarters, capers and olives. Sprinkle parsley over all and drizzle with *Dijon Dressing*.

Serves 2.

Dijon Dressing

1 clove GARLIC, crushed
1/2 tsp. DIJON MUSTARD
3 Tbsp. EXTRA VIRGIN OLIVE OIL
2 Tbsp. LEMON JUICE or RICE VINEGAR
SALT and fresh ground PEPPER to taste

In a small bowl, combine dressing ingredients and mix well.

Peanut Coated Orange Roughy

1 lb. ORANGE ROUGHY FILLETS
1/4 lb. SALTED PEANUTS, finely chopped
1/4 cup FLOUR
1/2 cup MILK
1 oz. BUTTER

Cut fillets into serving-size pieces. Combine peanuts with flour. Dip fish pieces into milk, then into peanut mixture, coating well. In a skillet, heat butter and cook fish 3-4 minutes per side. Drain and serve.

Serves 4.

About Orange Roughy

Orange Roughy brandish a bright orange skin and a pearly white flesh. They are low in fat and mild in flavor.

Sensationally Simple Orange Roughy

4 (1/4 lb. ea.) ORANGE ROUGHY FILLETS
1/4 cup BUTTER, softened
JUICE of 1/2 LEMON
LEMON PEPPER to taste
GARLIC SALT to taste
Cooked RICE
LEMON WEDGES

Cover baking sheet with aluminum foil. Arrange fillets in a single layer and dot each with butter. Squeeze lemon juice over all. Season with lemon pepper and garlic salt. Broil fillets for approximately 5 minutes or until fish is opaque and flakes easily with a fork. Serve with rice; garnish with lemon wedges.

Fish Stocks, Sauces, Butters & Batters

The following recipes can be used to enhance your seafood dining experience; some are integral components of the dish preparation, others are complementary accompaniments.

Court-Bouillon

2 lbs. FISH HEADS, BONES and TRIMMINGS
6 cups WATER
1 cup DRY WHITE WINE
2 ONIONS, thinly sliced
2 LEEKS, white part only, thinly sliced
2 Tbsp. WHITE WINE VINEGAR
2 strips (3-inch ea.) ORANGE PEEL
2 BAY LEAVES
1 tsp. FENNEL SEEDS
2 tsp. SALT

In a 6-quart saucepan, combine all ingredients and bring to a boil. Partially cover pan and cook over low heat for 30 minutes. Strain mixture through a sieve into a bowl, pressing out liquids from vegetables and fish with a spoon. Store in refrigerator for several days or freeze.

Poaching Court-Bouillon

1 qt. WATER
1 cup DRY WHITE WINE, or 1/4 cup WHITE WINE VINEGAR
1/2 ONION, or 2 GREEN ONIONS, sliced
2-3 sprigs PARSLEY
1 BAY LEAF
12 PEPPERCORNS, cracked
1/4 tsp. ANISE, FENNEL SEED or a small sprig of TARRAGON

In a saucepan, combine all ingredients. Bring to a boil and simmer for 15-20 minutes. Strain. May be frozen for future use.

Fish Stock

5 lbs. LEAN FISH HEADS, BONES and TRIMMINGS
2 Tbsp. BUTTER or OIL
1 cup diced ONION
1 cup diced CARROT
8 sprigs PARSLEY
1/2 BAY LEAF
1/2 cup MUSHROOM STEMS
1 tsp. WHITE PEPPERCORNS
1 1/2 cups DRY WHITE WINE

Wash fish parts well. Chop into chunks and soak in cold water to cover. Melt butter in a large stockpot over low heat. Add onion and carrot and sauté, covered, until soft but not browned. Drain fish parts and add to pot. Add remaining ingredients and water, to cover. Bring to a boil, reduce heat to low and simmer, uncovered, for 30 minutes, skimming surface occasionally. Do not boil. Strain through a fine sieve or cheesecloth; refrigerate or freeze until ready to use.

Clarified/Drawn Butter

Heat unsalted **BUTTER** very slowly; skim foam from top and pour or skim the clear (clarified) butter into a serving container. Clarified butter is often served in a chafing dish.

White or Béchamel Sauce

Very Thin:

| 1 Tbsp. BUTTER | 1/2 Tbsp. FLOUR | 1 cup HOT MILK |

Thin:

| 1 Tbsp. BUTTER | 1 Tbsp. FLOUR | 1 cup HOT MILK |

Medium:

| 2 Tbsp. BUTTER | 2 Tbsp. FLOUR | 1 cup HOT MILK |

Thick:

| 2 Tbsp. BUTTER | 3-4 Tbsp. FLOUR | 1 cup HOT MILK |

Very Thick:

| 2 1/2 tsp. BUTTER | 4-5 Tbsp. FLOUR | 1 cup HOT MILK |

Melt the butter in a heavy saucepan. Stir in flour and cook, stirring constantly, until the paste cooks and bubbles. Do not let brown. Add hot milk, continuing to stir as the sauce thickens. Bring to a boil. Add **SALT** and **PEPPER** to taste, lower heat and cook, stirring, for 2-4 minutes more.

Note: To cool sauce for later use, cover it with wax paper or pour a film of milk over top to prevent a skin from forming.

Pepper Sauce

1 Tbsp. OLIVE OIL
1/3 cup chopped ONIONS
1 Tbsp. minced fresh CHILE PEPPER
1 clove GARLIC, minced
3/4 cup chopped RED BELL PEPPER
1 tsp. PAPRIKA
1/2 tsp. RED HOT PEPPER SAUCE
1 tsp. WORCESTERSHIRE SAUCE
1 tsp. MUSTARD
1 tsp. RED WINE VINEGAR
1 Tbsp. LEMON JUICE

In a small skillet, heat oil. Add onions, chile pepper and garlic. Sauté over medium heat for 4-5 minutes. In a blender, combine sautéed vegetables and remaining ingredients. Purée until smooth (about 1 minute on high). Cover and refrigerate overnight to blend flavors.

Cocktail Sauce

JUICE of 1/2 LIME
1 Tbsp. CHILI SAUCE
1 Tbsp. WORCESTERSHIRE SAUCE
1/2 cup KETCHUP
3 tsp. HORSERADISH
1 1/2 tsp. WASABI (Japanese horseradish)
2 tsp. dehydrated ONIONS or fresh minced ONIONS

In a medium bowl, combine all ingredients. Chill thoroughly before serving with your favorite seafood.

Tartar Sauce

1 cup MAYONNAISE
1 Tbsp. minced ONION
3 Tbsp. minced DILL PICKLES
1 Tbsp. minced fresh PARSLEY

Mix all ingredients thoroughly; chill. Serve with your favorite seafood.

Makes 1 cup.

Sauce Tartare

1/2 Tbsp. finely chopped CAPERS
1/2 Tbsp. finely chopped PICKLE
1/2 Tbsp. finely chopped PARSLEY
1/2 Tbsp. finely chopped ONION
1 cup MAYONNAISE

Combine all ingredients lightly and chill.

Sauce Soubise

1 cup THICK WHITE SAUCE (see p. 84)
1/3 cup finely chopped SPANISH ONION

In a saucepan, prepare *Thick White Sauce,* sautéing Spanish onion in butter for 3 minutes, then continue with rest of *Thick White Sauce* instructions.

Red Butter Sauce

1 cup chopped SHALLOTS
2 cups RED WINE
2 BAY LEAVES
1/4 cup HEAVY CREAM
2 lbs. BUTTER, at room temperature, sliced
SALT and PEPPER to taste

In a saucepan over high heat, combine shallots, red wine and bay leaves. Cook until wine is almost completely reduced. Add cream and cook until slightly reduced. Lower heat to medium. Whisk in butter, one slice at a time until all has melted. Season with salt and pepper. Remove bay leaves before serving.

Basil, Dill or Tarragon Butter

1 Tbsp. LEMON JUICE
1 Tbsp. BUTTER, melted
1 Tbsp. fresh BASIL, DILL or TARRAGON
SALT and PEPPER to taste

In a small bowl, combine all ingredients except salt and pepper and mix thoroughly. Drizzle flavored butter over your favorite seafood then sprinkle with salt and pepper before baking, grilling, etc.

Seafood Pesto

1 lb. BASIL LEAVES
5-6 cloves GARLIC, minced
1 Tbsp. COARSE SALT
1 cup grated PARMESAN CHEESE
2 oz. PIMENTO
1/4 tsp. BLACK PEPPER
1 cup OLIVE OIL

Wash basil leaves and pat dry. Blend all ingredients together except olive oil. Slowly work olive oil into the mixture. Serve warm or chilled.

Beurre Blanc Sauce

(White Butter Sauce)

6 oz. WHITE WINE
3 oz. WHITE WINE VINEGAR
3 WHOLE BLACK PEPPERCORNS
1 SHALLOT, cut into quarters
1 cup HEAVY CREAM
6 oz. cold UNSALTED BUTTER, cut into pieces
3 oz. cold BUTTER, cut into pieces

Combine wine, vinegar, peppercorns and shallot in a saucepan. Reduce to 1-2 tablespoons and the consistency of syrup. Add cream and reduce again to 4 tablespoons and very thick. Remove pan from heat. Add butters, approximately 2 ounces at a time, stirring constantly and allowing each piece to melt before adding more. Strain and keep warm until ready to use.

Makes 1/2 cup sauce.

Note: This sauce may be flavored with orange, lemon, spice, herbs, berry or fruit concentrates. These may be added at the end or during the reduction of the cream.

Rémoulade Sauce

1 1/2 cups MAYONNAISE
2 tsp. grated LEMON PEEL
2 Tbsp. finely chopped fresh PARSLEY
Pinch of CAYENNE
1 tsp. ANCHOVY PASTE
1/4 cup finely chopped DILL PICKLES
1 Tbsp. CAPERS
2 HARD-BOILED EGGS, chopped

Mix all ingredients together and blend well. Serve with your favorite seafood.

Makes 2 cups.

Hollandaise Sauce

3 EGG YOLKS
1 Tbsp. LEMON JUICE
1 stick BUTTER (no substitutes)

In a 2 qt. saucepan, stir egg yolks and lemon juice vigorously. Add 1/4 of the butter and heat over very low heat, stirring constantly with a wire whisk until butter has melted. Add remaining butter, 1/4 stick at a time until all butter has melted and sauce has thickened. To make *Mousseline Sauce,* just before serving, beat **1/4 cup HEAVY WHIPPING CREAM** in a chilled bowl until stiff and fold into *Hollandaise Sauce.*

Orange Marmalade Soy Sauce

1/3 cup ORANGE MARMALADE
1/4 cup LEMON JUICE
1/4 cup SOY SAUCE
1 clove GARLIC, minced
1/8 tsp. GINGER
1 tsp. CORNSTARCH

In a small saucepan, combine all ingredients and mix well. Cook, stirring constantly, until clear and thickened. Serve hot or cold with seafoods.

Walnut Fish Batter

1/4 cup very fine CRACKER CRUMBS
3/4 cup FLOUR
2 EGG WHITES
1 cup small-chopped WALNUTS

Combine cracker crumbs with flour in a shallow dish. In a bowl, beat egg whites until stiff then place in a second shallow dish. Place walnut meats in a third shallow dish. Dip one-inch slices of fish into flour mixture, egg white and walnut dishes to coat. Fry or grill until well done.

Cornmeal Batter

1 EGG
1 Tbsp. WATER
3/4 cup FLOUR

1/4 cup YELLOW CORNMEAL
1 tsp. SALT
1/8 tsp. PEPPER

In a medium bowl, beat egg with water. In a shallow dish, combine flour, cornmeal, salt and pepper. Dip seafood into egg mixture, coat with cornmeal mixture and deep fry until golden brown.

Tempura Batter

2 EGG YOLKS   1 cup WATER   1 cup FLOUR

Place egg yolks in a bowl; gradually stir in water and beat with a fork. Slowly beat in flour; batter should be slightly lumpy. Dip seafood into batter and fry or bake until golden brown.

Bread Crumb Batter

1 cup FLOUR
1 tsp. SALT
1/8 tsp. PEPPER

2 EGGS
1 cup dry BREAD CRUMBS

In a shallow bowl, mix flour, salt and pepper. In another shallow bowl, beat eggs lightly. Coat seafood with flour mixture, dip into eggs, then roll in bread crumbs. Fry or bake until browned.

Beer Batter

1 cup FLOUR
1/2 tsp. SALT

1/8 tsp. PEPPER
3/4 cup FLAT BEER

In a medium bowl, combine dry ingredients; gradually stir in beer and beat mixture until creamy. Coat seafood with batter and fry in hot oil until golden brown.

Index

Index (Continued)

Index (Continued)

Index (Continued)

FLORIDA COOK BOOK

Straight from the Sunshine State, over 100 favorite recipes! Try *Aunt Sally's Key Lime Pie, Piña Colada Muffins, Seminole Pumpkin Fry Bread* or seafood delights like *Sautéed Gulf Coast Grouper, Drunken Shrimp* and *Pompano Baked in Sour Cream Sauce.* Includes historical as well as modern trivia and a guide to Florida's food festivals.

5 1/2 x 8 1/2 — 96 pages . . . $6.95

NORTH CAROLINA COOK BOOK

Filled with family favorites as well as recipes that showcase North Carolina's specialty foods. *Sausage Pinwheels, Shipwrecked Crab, Scuppernong Grape Butter, Carolina Blender Slaw, North Carolina Pork BBQ, Rock Fish Muddle, Hushpuppy Fritters, Hummingbird Cake, Peanut Butter Pie* . . . and more!

5 1/2 x 8 1/2 — 96 pages . . . $6.95

VIRGINIA COOK BOOK

Savory ham dishes, delicious apple recipes, tempting peanut delights and a cornucopia of historical and family favorites. Recipes that reflect the many flavors of Virginia and highlight its celebrated heritage. Includes interesting Virginia facts and a guide to Virginia's food festivals.

5 1/2 x 8 1/2 — 96 pages . . . $6.95

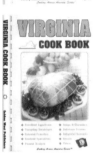

OREGON COOK BOOK

Over 200 great recipes from the beautiful state of Oregon! Tasty treats from the kitchens of dignitaries, homemakers and Bed-and-Breakfasts. Sample the flavors of Oregon with *Hazelnut Stuffed Chicken Breast, Tillamook Seafood & Cheese Linguine* and *Earthquake Cake!* Includes interesting Oregon facts and festivals.

5 1/2 x 8 1/2 — 128 Pages . . . $6.95

WASHINGTON COOK BOOK

This book captures the wonderful and tantalizing diversity of this scenic West Coast state. Over 185 recipes from Washington's dignitaries, fine restaurants, chefs (including Graham Kerr), cozy inns and homemakers. Entire section devoted to Northwestern seafood. Includes trivia about the entire state, its festivals and landmarks.

5 1/2 x 8 1/2 — 128 Pages . . . $6.95

EASY RECIPES for
WILD GAME AND FISH

By hunter-traveler-cook Ferne Holmes. More than 200 "wild" recipes for large and small game, wild fowl, fish and side dishes.

5 1/2 x 8 1/2 — 160 Pages . . . $6.95

BEST BARBECUE RECIPES

A collection of more than 200 taste-tempting recipes. • Sauces • Rubs • Marinades • Mops • Ribs • Wild Game • Fish and Seafood • Pit barbecue and more!

5 1/2 x 8 1/2 — 144 pages . . . $6.95

SALSA LOVERS COOK BOOK

More than 180 taste-tempting recipes for salsas that will make every meal a special event! Salsas for salads, appetizers, main dishes and desserts! Put some salsa in your life! More than 200,000 copies in print!

5 1/2 x 8 1/2—128 pages . . . $6.95

BERRY LOVERS COOK BOOK

Over 120 delicious recipes featuring flavorful and nutritious berries! Try *Blueberry Buttermilk Muffins, Strawberry Peach Meringue Pie, Raspberry Dream Bars, Blackberry Summer Salad* or *Boysenberry Mint Frosty* and many more. Tempting recipes for all occasions. Includes berry facts and trivia!

5 1/2 x 8 1/2 — 96 pages . . . $6.95

VEGGIE LOVERS COOK BOOK

Everyone will love these no-cholesterol, no-animal recipes! Over 200 nutritious, flavorful recipes by Chef Morty Star. Includes a foreword by Dr. Michael Klaper. Nutritional analysis for each recipe to help you plan a healthy diet.

5 1/2 x 8 1/2 — 128 pages . . . $6.95

ORDER BLANK
GOLDEN WEST PUBLISHERS

 4113 N. Longview Ave. • Phoenix, AZ 85014

www.goldenwestpublishers.com • **1-800-658-5830** • FAX 602-279-6901

Qty	Title	Price	Amount
	Apple Lovers Cook Book	**6.95**	
	Bean Lovers Cook Book	**6.95**	
	Berry Lovers Cook Book	**6.95**	
	Best Barbecue Recipes	**6.95**	
	Chili-Lovers' Cook Book	**6.95**	
	Citrus Lovers Cook Book	**6.95**	
	Corn Lovers Cook Book	**6.95**	
	Easy Recipes for Wild Game & Fish	**6.95**	
	Florida Cook Book	**6.95**	
	Joy of Muffins	**6.95**	
	Low Fat Mexican Recipes	**6.95**	
	North Carolina Cook Book	**6.95**	
	Oregon Cook Book	**6.95**	
	Quick-Bread Cook Book	**6.95**	
	Salsa Lovers Cook Book	**6.95**	
	Seafood Lovers Cook Book	**6.95**	
	Take This Chile & Stuff It!	**6.95**	
	Veggie Lovers Cook Book	**6.95**	
	Virginia Cook Book	**6.95**	
	Washington Cook Book	**6.95**	
Shipping & Handling Add ⇒	U.S. & Canada	$3.00	
	Other countries	$5.00	

☐ My Check or Money Order Enclosed $

☐ MasterCard   ☐ VISA ($20 credit card minimum)

(Payable in U.S. funds)

Acct. No.   Exp. Date

Signature

Name   Telephone

Address

City/State/Zip

Call for a FREE catalog of all of our titles

02/02   **This order blank may be photocopied**   Seafood Lovers